Dedicated to my great friend and supporter Eddy French for believing in me.

And in memory of Rockstar the goat, Atticus the chicken, Wallie the dog, Zainy the pig, Fiona the cow, Gizmo the dog, Shelagh the lobster, Esther The Wonder Pig and Aries the sheep.

Rest in sweet, peaceful pastures, my friends.

Contents

The Animal in Me

A memoir of a lifetime of being with animals

Billy Thompson

The Conrad Press

The Animal in Me

Published by The Conrad Press in the United Kingdom 2024

Tel: +44(0)1227 472 874
www.theconradpress.com
info@theconradpress.com

ISBN 978-1-916966-16-1

Typesetting and Cover Design by: Levellers

The Conrad Press logo was designed by Maria Priestley.

Printed and bound in Great Britain by Clays Ltd, Elcograf S.p.A.

Preface

The animal in me is the sequel to the first part of my memoirs, *Earth Boy*. I believe everyone is born kind. With my writings I've tried to rekindle the great love we all had for all creatures when we were young. It really doesn't take much to reconnect with what modern-day life makes us shut away.

Open your eyes and heart together to see your story of kindness unfold in front of you.

Relax, breathe – there's no need for your heart to be hard. Be kind, it's easy.

The Animal in Me

Chapter One: The magic of animals

Animals will never disappoint you – in fact, they will only ever enhance your life. Each one is an individual work of living art, a miracle of life. This paragraph was how I started to conclude my first book, *Earth Boy*. I had wanted to rekindle that love we all remember having for animals (even the tiniest mini beast) as children.

We never forget our first pet's name and the pain of heartbreak of our loss at their simple burial, their graves marked with a cross made of lolly sticks and a hand-written name. We remember our first soft animal toy with endearment and cruelty to animals was a thing of monsters. Proving the importance of that very special and loving bond, even your bank now uses your first pet's name as a security question.

The expressions of animals speak volumes, and if you take the time to observe and learn their hidden languages, your very own animal magnetism will start to appear. With my heart and eyes wide opened I celebrate my partnership with kindness every day. I'm fully tuned in and my receptive satellites for any creature's communications never miss an opportunity to learn more. The most damaged creatures will in time turn around and trust humans again.

There's no 'it's not working', just failed or phoney attempts at supporting the animal to regain the confidence in themselves to heal and lead a happy and content life. Just as a good workman never blames his tools, or a good therapist never blames their clients for taking time to recover, a good rescuer never blames the animals asking for help in front of him. It may sound like the oldest cliché in the world, but time is, of course, a great healer. It's our magic wand when showing animals it's okay to trust again. It costs nothing, and is easily and readily available if you are disciplined enough to plan to suit the animal's needs each day (or to accept that your environment is not the winning formula for this animal), and to accept the help offered and available all around you.

I've always loved getting lost in nature, mentally or physically. Be it gardening, climbing trees, sitting quietly on a hill watching flying birds, wild swimming or just getting lost with my dogs on a desolated winter beach walk. Something amazing always happens, whether it be noticing a seal appear while I'm swimming, or the newly-constructed wren's nest tucked into the roof beams while I'm out sitting still, or simply the beginning of a rose bug starting its journey to full bloom while I'm gardening.

All things earthly have interested me ever since I can remember and Mother Nature has always been by my side, she's taught me so much. Her gentle whispers in my ear lead me to look up at exactly the right time to notice a little piece of wonderfulness. Solitary bumblebees disappearing down holes just their size, and the first flight of the blue tit family from my garden bird boxes. The breath-taking starling murmurations are a reminder of just how magical Mother Nature and her family are. Her most important lesson to us all is to stop and stare, stand around and watch and listen because out in the wilderness, every day is a magnificent school day.

The smaller underrated things in life often give the best advice. They teach us respect, they show us that other lives have purpose and are just as important: yes, that's right, just as important. Look how ants work together their intricate communities all working for the same common goal, a collective responsibility, survival of their colony – so don't allow your children to jump on them, wiping out these hard-working creatures. Teach your children to respect all life, no matter how small

I remember hearing for the first time the importance of earthworms and how they channel oxygen down below the surface, supporting healthy soil, and that the biting mosquito is just a mother collecting food for her babies. These snippets of Mother Nature's secrets filled me with an appetite for learning more and more about them. Finding a feather on the ground could catapult my thoughts into the beautiful world of the unknown. I would start to imagine who it belonged to, a kind of guess-the-bird test that would tease my knowledge. You can only marvel at the natural world. It's real-life magic.

I've been able to apply so many of Mother Nature's lessons in my rescue work, such as gentleness, patience, observation, body language, intuition, leadership, self-belief and self-healing. Endless scientific reports explain the positive effects of spending time in nature. We can read about how stroking animals brings down dangerously high blood pressure (a hidden killer), of how PAT (pets as therapy) animals can bring comfort to life-limited people, and now there are even dogs who are trained to detect illness and bring about early diagnosis and life-saving treatments for humans. Volunteering in the great outdoors with animals even has positive effects on poor mental health and almost immediately lowers crippling anxiety levels.

What would life be like for us without animals? Unimaginable, bland and loveless. Maybe for the reader who doesn't get a good daily helping of fur, feathers, shell or scales will not understand the benefits of what they are missing but by the time you've finished this book I know your outlook will be different. I will take you on a journey of kindness which will make even the darkest of hearts fall in love with the magic of animals.

Whilst on the beautiful isle of St Thomas's in the West Indies on Christmas Eve 2021, I received the sad news from my great nephew Charlie (Dogbite) that Murray Mint, a horse I had shared a family bond with for twenty-seven years was put to sleep that morning back in the UK. Murray's life had come to an end due to his old age combined with a neurological problem.

Murray was only a tiny week-old foal when I rescued him almost three decades ago. In my eyes, he was perfect. He had bright eyes and long, thin legs with a white sock from the knee down. He was almost all black, apart from a long wide blaze of white that ran down his face from top to bottom, and a splash of white the size of a melon on his tummy. His only sin was to be born the wrong sex and the wrong colour.

You might think this is ludicrous, that surely a baby is a baby and all foals are beautiful. Unfortunately, just like in certain parts of the world where female human babies are not wanted as much as males, this is a major problem in animal rescue right now. Male foals, especially those born mainly black or with some white (piebalds), are not wanted by certain unscrupulous 'horse breeders'. Male foals are rounded up from their herds and separated from their mums (like dairy cows), sometimes as young as a day old. They are worthless in the eyes of their betrayer and dumped, left to die. Sometimes the mothers are removed, and a similar fate awaits the babies.

I was once called to rescue seven male foals all under four weeks old dumped in one field, starving, wet and cold, left to perish. Murray's mum had already been taken away.

'It's now or never,' the so-called breeder said to me. 'Take him.'

The problem was that on my outreach visits, I was

quite often dropped off on site, typically with only one vehicle, and left for hours to help the animals. My work consisted of anti-parasite solutions for blood sucking lice and mites as well as treatments for internal worm burden, minor wound cleaning, insect repellents, health checks and the offer of full veterinary help free of charge (by our own obliging vet) if any of those animals needed it. I would also take away any unwanted animals without passing judgement, a kind of animal amnesty. In those days there was the added complication of having no mobile phones. On this day, I thankfully had two great helpers, Lara and Jo, and our decision-making process was quick. Collectively we agreed that we needed to walk Murray home, or lose the opportunity to save him. We thought walking home could take approximately three hours; we could possibly find a pay phone and call for help, or my lift would eventually catch up with us. This was not to be the case, and so between the three of us we encouraged our new baby with half sucked Murray Mints, kisses, tender massages, a few lifts and pushes. We walked across fields, up and over hills, crossed running streams and made our way through woodland. We made king-Chairs when Murray just stopped, lifting his rear end to carry him along. We played catch-up while the boiled sweets lasted, and made enthusiastic horse noises to quicken his pace. Sometimes our baby would just stop, and nothing we did could move him. After more than five hours, we were too exhausted to carry him. We would rest until a little life returned to our new youngster, and off we would run again.

Six hours later we returned home, exhausted. For Murray's first night he would bed down in the lounge on a pile of duvets along with me and many of our other rescued family. I gave him two-hourly milk feeds which took huge amounts of encouragement, warm milk tipping

13

onto my fingers as I taught him to suckle the artificial teat of the bottle. When he finished, I would quietly crawl away to fall asleep on the sofa, but it wouldn't be long before he climbed onto me. With his tummy now full, Murray would soon be in a deep sleep, weighing down on me. As he relaxed and stretched out the length of me, I watched his eyelids, ears and lips twitch along with his dreams. I, on the other hand, was unable to breathe, struggling to find a position I could fall asleep in without disturbing him.

I'm sure he thought about and fretted for his mother, but he knew his survival was in the large bottles of milk I offered him – a built-in self-preservation plan, I guess. Murray accepted my love and kindness and very quickly I became his mum, his protection and his herd. Rearing any baby creature, they will always respond to your love. I've done so many times with foal, calf, lamb, wild boar, piglet, deer, fox, squirrel, kitten, puppy, mouse, rat and bird; all were won over with the comfort of love. Love is a universal language with all babies. You don't need to say a word with your lips. Hold them tight and let them feel your heartbeat and listen to your slow, deep breath. That's all it will take to get them through their first night with you. When you have provided the very best in resources, comfort and support, there's no doubt your baby will only thrive. Each different species will need a tailored individual nursing plan; there's no one-size-fits-all solution so don't make any assumptions. It just takes good old-fashioned research.

Imprinting is inevitable with newborns and newly hatched creatures. If a domestic animal or bird is going to stay with you forever, there aren't any major problems ahead. Wild animals should be treated differently so they can be returned to the wild without attachment issues; a wild animal trying to seek human contact with the wrong people could face many hazards. It doesn't take long to end up with a thriving or strapping strong young animal on your hands so be prepared.

It wasn't long before Murray started to give you his paw like the dogs would for a biscuit. With each growth spurt Murray moved out of the house into the garden and eventually into a stable with a paddock with his brother José (another orphaned black and white male foal). Murray and José were inseparable even when asleep their bodies either crossed each other or leant up against one another. They could be sunbathing in a massive field but one piece of each other would always be touching the other. The honour of being Murray and José Mum, Dad, family and herd (whatever you want to call our powerful bond) has been one of my greatest privileges. The years in between have been filled with incredible memories, built on the unique friendship both horses bequeathed upon me.

These and thousands of other interspecies unions have given me the insight to develop the skillset to continue to help, save and care for many of life's forgotten creatures. Murray's story and his life touched so many people. His incredible journey and his amazing love for humans meant everyone who met him simply loved him. He taught people so much, achieving deep personal bonds especially with his communicating tools that were better with humans than other equines. Murray was a special ambassador for the unridden horse. He led the way in showing another way for loving the horse without the need to sit on his back. This way was for a fair and uniquely balanced friendship, starting with the mass of unlearning most of us 'horse people' are too scared to face.

My work under The Flair Foundation (a group I started back in the nineties to help animals, especially horses living on traveller sites) for theses invisible foals and their sad mother's misery will not end until the people responsible for breeding these animals stop for good. José and I never stop talking about 'our Murray'. In fact, not a single conversation with the horses happens without including his name. Just the mention of the legendary M-word brings ears forward and wide eyes among our trusted herd of devoted Murray followers.

Without a doubt there's a big black clumsy cob galloping about to the tune of *Champion the Wonder Horse* in heaven now, one who thinks he's a delicate and graceful unicorn; who I know will put a smile on even the most straight-laced and dignified angel's face. Goodnight, Mr Murray Mint.

Chapter Two: Flair's Foundation

Horses were my first large-close-contact-animal-friendship. A kid from the metropolis, I found them majestic creatures, everything about them just magical. From their familiar smell to their magical size, I would find myself overwhelmed with every new discovery. Each fallen tooth, horseshoe or knot of mane; I collected it all and treasured the world I found myself in. It would be years before I got to live the dream of sharing my life with cows, pigs, sheep and goats and learn of their amazing qualities and companionship too.

My first 'real' equine was a New Forest Cross pony (almost a horse at 14.2hh). He was all brown (bay) apart from his white blaze that ran down his soft face, fading at his left nostril. He was more than twenty years old and an unwanted wilful and still very strong bullet. At the time of Flair being given away, I was looking after my sister's very own pony, Bess, a 13.2hh grey Connemara mare. In fact, my sister Lil got her own pony far sooner than I did. Flair's owner had looked at me and said, 'Animal Man, do you want a pony? Free to a good home.' How could I refuse?

Flair was far too strong for most teenagers my age. He was also extremely fast and jumped anything put in front of him, including stable doors and field gates. Flair was my dream friend and even though I rode a lot back then, even time sitting with him in the field or relaxing together in his stable was an out of world experience for this 'towny kid'.

I had a part-time job working in a pub kitchen on Chislehurst Common in Kent, which dragged me away from our exciting escapades. This was long before I got my driving licence, so I rode Flair to work where he spent the four hours I worked mowing the pub's lawn. The owner of the pub didn't particularly like me or Flair, but I was cheap labour. I think 'the boy on the horse' stole his thunder, because I was often greeted with a warm welcome by the pub's regular customers, while he was side-stepped. His beady eye kept watch over me so I didn't detract from my role and play with the pony.

Flair was definitely a distraction. On one occasion, I was asked to chill some champagne for a function later that day. Instead of laying out the bottles in the cooler, I put them in the freezer. Later that afternoon the two dozen bottles of fizz exploded, to the screams of the whole kitchen and restaurant teams as they ran for cover – whoops.

After each shift, I was summoned by the authoritarian landlord to the many piles of Flair's droppings. He watched over me while I cleared away the very last of my pony's very own calling card. The pub clients took us into their hearts and would stay all afternoon in the garden, enthralled – how many other pubs had a big shaggy lawnmower? A quick tack-up and we would be on our way.

I rode to the common and up through the woods and bridleways to make our way back to the stables. The last straw (if you'll excuse the pun) for the landlord with my employment came when I arrived at work on Flair after being caught in a torrential downpour. I couldn't leave Flair in the garden with the dark clouds still raining bucketloads upon us. Instead I settled my soaking-wet pony in the garage of Chislehurst's very own Genghis Khan, alongside his shining new Jaguar sheltering from the elements. With a few full-body shakes to dry himself, off Flair sent a healthy coating of wet steaming horsehair over my boss's pride and joy. It was like a scene from the Thelwell Cartoons of hairy little ponies in all sorts of naughty situations. Even for me, it was hard to distinguish whether the garage was home to one or two shaggy wet dobbins. When I suggested to the landlord that his car might be the hairiest of the pair, his face reddened to an even deeper shade.

'I never want to see you or that *thing* again.' It was the last thing he ever muttered to me. Poor Flair. My former boss had made himself perfectly clear that I should leave and not return, so I tacked up my bedraggled buddy and rode out of The Rose and Crown for the very last time.

Every hour I spent with my ponies, I learned huge amounts from them and dreamed of one day helping to save many more of them from the 'lifetime responsibility' they face, even in good homes. Many family horses are treated like sports equipment. When people decide they want a faster one, they'll sell them on like they would a motorbike or jet-ski. Sadly, the illusion that the beloved family pony, who kept the children safe for years, would always be safe herself, so often proved not to be the case. The myth that they'll spend the rest of their life with another 'devoted' family is a reality as rare as hen's teeth. Most children outgrow and sell on their 'best friend', and the cycle continues until the pony is seen to be old and financially worthless. In the end, many family ponies end up in unscrupulous situations when they should instead be facing a happy, well-earned retirement, rather than the dealer's gun and their flesh and bones becoming food for zoo animals.

I rescued a wonderful pony, who I named Fanny the Wonder Horse. Using her identification-mark, I traced thirteen of her previous registered keepers. None of them were the least bit bothered that I had taken her from the 'knackersman', whose job was to slaughter horses. Not a single one of these 'owners' showed a trace of gratitude for the lifeline we had offered this kind and gentle lady.

I had other ideas, ways of finding a forever home for the seniors in need of a secure retirement plan, one that rewarded their loyal service and gave them the care and attention they needed in their later years. Big dreams for a young boy.

I never failed to provide for my pony. He was my world, my heartbeat. It was an unbelievable miracle that I should ever be lucky enough to have my very own pony. My parents had instilled it in my sister and I that if you take on a companion animal, you will always look after them – no giving up and no giving in. 'There's no such word as can't,' Mum would always say. No matter what Flair needed, he would get, right up until the very last day of his forty-two years of life. Every birthday, Christmas and other special occasions, he either got a can of Tizer or Guinness – his two favourite drinks – and each of my packed lunches contained a treat for him, too.

If you'll allow it, the creatures you share your life with will interlink with you. Deep bonds, unequalled anywhere, will flourish and brighten each and every day. It doesn't take much for something incredible to develop, and before long you'll be reading each other like a book. I have no doubt that animals love us just like our human families do. You'll understand this if you're ready to accept just how powerful these interdependent relationships are. After all, is anybody really disputing the fact that other animals are sentient?

Flair's death hurt me deep down in my soul. After he passed, I decided that something great should be born from our long and happy union. I wanted to do more for equines in his name. I wanted our boy-and-pony relationship to grow up into something mature – a local resource in helping horses and ponies in poor situations, be it tethered, old, neglected or unwanted ones. In his name I started The Flair Foundation, a local group of feeders and carers who would network and support the needs of unfortunate horses and ponies that we would hear about. To those who needed help but would not surrender their equines to us, we would provide everything completely free of charge. Their part of the bargain was that they would learn from us and bond with their animal, beginning to understand the individual responsibility that comes with keeping any creature. We, too, needed to build professional working relationships with the people we didn't understand. It was the beginning of a journey, and from it an amazing legacy in the name of my dear first pony was born.

Chapter Three: The officers' mess

After I was fabulously fired for taking my pony to work, I needed to find another job, fast. I searched the job ads in the local newspapers and quickly found a post working as a waiter inside a large barracks in Woolwich South East London. I was now only seventeen and a half years old and desperately needed the dosh.

The building which housed the operation was famous for being the largest fronted army barracks in Europe, and had also suffered two IRA terrorist attack back in the 1980s. The 300-year-old grade two listed building was called The Royal Artillery Barracks. It was home to many military functions for hundreds of people. Many high-ranking military officers attended, as well as Queen Elizabeth II.

In my new role I worked four shifts a week, a mix of

morning, lunch and dinner posts. Each shift required me to dress in the full silver service attire of black trousers, white shirt, a bow tie, cumber belt, black waistcoat and well-polished shoes. I was mainly there to set up each meal to feed the officers and serve them what they wanted. After breakfast, I would refill their coffees in the comfortable officers' mess. There would be late shifts too, when the barracks entertained and the function rooms with their huge statues and works of art would be set up to receive hundreds of guests. We even had a beautifully unused toilet just for Her Majesty should she need to spend her very own penny. This WC was strictly out of bounds to anyone other than QE2, and we were all regularly warned accordingly. I even enquired once as to whether it was possible to have a look at what a royal lavatory looks like (perhaps a diamond-crusted seat and velvety crown-printed toilet tissue, protected by a beefeater?). I was given a firm 'no', and the room remained locked with a key, which hung on a ceremonial rope, from a gold hook in my manager Brenda's office. (As I've just now mentioned Her Majesty our late queen, and as the satirical magazine *Private Eye* used to refer to Her Majesty as 'Brenda', can I please emphasise for the avoidance of any doubt, that 'Brenda' here refers to my boss, not Her Majesty.)

I was on my first breakfast shift when I spotted a kitten looking for food outside the main kitchen. I watched on until I could help myself to a plate of goodies for the tiny homeless bunch. I placed a fake order with the breakfast chefs, and nobody queried an officers' meal. I collected the feast and placed the piled-up plate down outside the building. Slowly, a whole gang arrived: six multi-coloured kittens – only weeks old and the size of grapefruits – and a skinny black cat (mum). They swallowed down mouthfuls of the A La Carte servings.

It soon became apparent that I would need to help find a suitable placement for this little family if they were to thrive. The cats weren't neutered, and had been introduced by the barracks to try and eradicate the rat-and-mice problem throughout the onsite buildings. No provision was in place to feed the cats, and if any of them needed the vet it was hard luck. The powers that be expected them to live off the rodents alone. As usual, I had other plans. Each shift, I turned up with kitten food, cat boxes and traps. The army guards on the gates searched each car, inside and out, and each civilian entering on foot was also searched. I was an anomaly, and the squaddies were a little shocked when I turned up with my animal paraphernalia. When I found homes for the kittens, I'd leave with them the same day. I would be waved through the queues of staff finishing their shifts. 'That's the mad animal man', I'd hear them say. Some officers called me St Francis of Artillery because I was always helping the cats or befriending the officers' horses. Now, I needed a safer place to house the mums and kittens who were living outside, still feeding their babies until they were old enough to leave mum for a new home. My partner in crime was Karen, the wife of a paratrooper and queen of naughtiness. Karen was in her mid-twenties and petite at just over five-foot-tall, but she had the spirit of a spitfire. We became known to our colleagues as the Dynamic Duo.

Karen suggested that we 'acquire' Lilibet's throne room and set up a nursery for the kittens. 'No one's going to look there, are they?' she went on. After all, the Queen rarely visited and had reportedly never used her very own regal loo. While Karen went off to work her magic, I was to raid housekeeping for bedding to set up the new nursery. Due to our joint shenanigans, boss Brenda would often call Karen and I in and demand us to rein in our double act, or else.

Karen had been a waitress since long before I arrived, and she and Brenda already shared a tense working relationship. 'Brenda hates me,' she always said – long before I arrived, it had been a battle of wills between them. Karen and I both got on well with the officers (even the difficult ones), and we enjoyed our job because every shift dissolved into a comedy sketch. Believe it or not, Karen's naughtiness was on another level, and my practical jokes would pale into insignificance compared with her outrageous behaviour.

On this occasion, I returned with armfuls of bedding and waited patiently outside Her Majesty's best kept secret. Within minutes, Karen was back with the key.

'How did you get that?' I asked.

'I went into Brenda's office with a mop and bucket,' Karen explained. 'I said, *I'm just going to give the royal toilet a once-over,* and I took the prized key from its hook. It was like taking candy from a baby.'

We prepared the space for the kittens with all sorts of beds, bowls and toys. The nursery took shape, and soon it was ready for its little princes and princesses. Karen and I were the nannies. The only problem now was the key, and how we would continue to access it each day to look after the 'kids'. As always, our modern day, female Houdini was ready to solve it with her very own optical illusion. She was to swap the key on the rope for another, while we kept hold of the monarch's key. Before we knew it, our royal kindergarten was fully up and running, and the babies thrived in our care. Each tiny individual got what they needed until we could find them fantastic homes in their own little palaces.

On one occasion, Karen and I were together playing kittens in HRH's water closet, when we heard footsteps and then a key being pushed into the keyhole. Outside, we could hear Brenda complaining to her latest clone that the key wouldn't turn. Karen and I were mortified, thinking it would be game over for us. Not only would the cats and kittens be homeless, but we would be fired too. Thankfully, our key was still in the lock on the inside, keeping us all safe. Brenda accepted the incident as possibly having been a feeble attempt at opening the door.

Later, Karen was called in and blamed for the incident, because Brenda remembered that she had been the last one to ask for the key. In revenge for yet another of Brenda's moans, our practical joker crossed the line again. The next time Karen cleaned the function room in preparation from an upcoming Officers' Ball, she used the ladder we used to clean the Chandelier to climb up to the 15ft white statues, which stood on plinths. She placed cucumber slices over each of their eyes, and capers in their ears, finishing off with a banana skin on each shoulder like military decoration.

It wasn't until the first serving during the event, as we all took our positions along the wall waiting to clear the officers' plates away, that a steaming mad Brenda looked up and noticed the new make-overs of the surrounding art pieces. With smoke coming out of her ears and an expression which indicated she was about to self-combust, she stared at Karen and I, but she had no proof that it was *our* creative skills that had brightened the place up. All the same, we were becoming increasingly aware that our time at the barracks was running out.

We had to quicken our pace to clear the mess of any casts left onsite. We began catching the adult cats, and I took them home. Brenda called us in, suspicious that we were interfering with 'army property', namely the cats, and warned us off getting involved in anything other than our job. She also pointed out that next month was a big

25

date in the barracks calendar, and told us we needed to up our game if we wanted to keep our jobs.

Inside the Officers' Mess stood a huge glass display case, which was about three metres long by two metres high. Inside were two mannequins dressed in safari gear, holding rifles behind a stuffed 'trophy' lion, who had been killed for fun (just like Cecil the protected lion, who was hunted in 2015 by American dentist Walter Palmer, and sadly took 24 hours to die). This was the officers' pride and joy, and was accompanied by a bear skin rug complete with opened, mouth, head and claws, laid out on the floor. The room was lit with standard lamps and filled with winged backed chairs and small tables for the officers' drinks. A couple of the more demanding officers would spend the evening here into the early hours, slowly getting drunk on their favourite single malt whiskeys and leaving the mess for us to clear away the next day. We soon learnt why it was called the Officers' Mess. I had debated with the older grumpy officers about how disrespectful the animal remains were, but they had just laughed me off. Now, it was time for the animals to get their own back.

One late winter shift, Karen and I came up with an idea. The Officers' Mess was quiet, with only three officers in. Two of them cared very little about the stuffed animals' original fate. After one left for bed, and the other two were either on the toilet or finding something to read, we set to work on our payback strategy.

Karen kicked her shoes off behind the display and climbed under the dead bear, while I removed a mannequin from the display and dressed in the Safari shorts and shirt, pulled the boots on, placed the wide hat on my head and took up the replica rifle. I climbed into position in the display case along with the lion and remaining mannequin and awaited my signal from the bear to play my part.

It wasn't long until an officer returned to his seat with another large whiskey and a hardback book. He sat perfectly in line with the bear skin on the floor facing him, and the hunting display case straight ahead of him. I stood and waited for my moment, as perfectly still as a sniper on a high-rise roof, focusing on his distant victim. I watched the officer turn the pages of the book and sip away at his nightcap.

Then came my signal: the bear starting to crawl across the floor towards a terrified and intoxicated officer. He was frozen in fear, unable to move. There was a loud thud as the hardback hit the floor, and his glass slipped into his lap. By now, the bear was beginning to stand up, and I lifted my rifle and pointed it through the glass at the petrified officer. His eyes widened, his mouth dropping in disbelief. I think he believed himself to be hallucinating. He was used to frontline battles, and bravely faced gunshots and shelling, but could take no more of his usual evening companions coming to life. His chair rolled back and threw him to the side. He scrambled for safety in the opposite direction, disappearing into the officers' live-in quarters. The bear and Safari Sam high-fived each other, huge grins on our faces.

We quickly tidied up the chair and wiped away the spilled whiskey. I poured another measure of whiskey into the glass and placed the hardback book by the side. We laid the bear back out, redressed the mannequin and fitted him back inside the display case. There was no longer a crime scene and anyone coming to investigated would find a perfectly ordered room. The Dynamic Duo returned to our workstation and prepared to finish our shift.

I had just collected the last two kittens from the royal nursery. As I took the stairs down to leave with my tiny black babies in their carry-box, I heard an array of excited voices down below.

A younger Captain from the group of four looked up. 'Seen any bears?' he said.

'Quick, to the armoury for the guns!' another shouted. 'Old Captain Ball's gone mad, thinks the bears are hunting us. We all laughed together.

'If only,' I whispered as I made my way out.

Chapter Four: The almighty one

Animal rescue is filled with highs and lows and even giving your 110% will sometimes not be enough. It's a real roller-coaster of emotions and you never know what each day will bring.

One incredible rescue consisted of a wonderfully kind couple called Emma and Simon finding a tiny egg, dropped from a nest two storeys up. The awaiting baby was starting to emerge from the cracked shell. Emma and Simon had taken turns to keep the broken egg warm on their journey to The Retreat. Like a pair of expecting parents, they spoke softly to their unborn, anticipating the arrival very soon.

As the tiny featherless baby pushed itself out of the other half of the egg (so small that baby and egg would have fitted on a ten pence piece) I could see there was a huge problem. The emerging joyful creature had a split the length of his abdomen, and his inner stomach was on the outside. I knew immediately that this was an emergency of very bad news, and explained to the shocked couple that this would spell disaster, and the only option was to sadly put the baby to sleep (euthanasia). After a very intense, long chat where the 'quality of life' argument had raised its head and died an immediate death, I drove the couple and baby to our vet.

Most vets we work with know we don't put animals to sleep easily – it's only ever after all other options have been investigated. Lauren the vet knew to do her best, examining the new-born who lay lifeless with fragments of shell still attached to his body. Her face said it all.

'Sadly, there's nothing I can do,' Lauren explained. Both Emma and Simon started to cry, their last traces of hope fading. I stared at the newly formed body now kicking his legs in defiance at the vet's prognosis.

'Please, try something,' I blurted, without thinking. 'He really wants to live.'

Lauren realised it was a make-or-break moment. 'Give me a minute,' she said, and took the baby out the back. Emma, Simon and I waited in uncertainty.

'It's incredible what vets can do these days,' I said, trying to comfort Emma and Simon. 'She'll have all the latest life-saving equipment out the back.' Creatures this young would usually stand little to no chance, but this little one had the best team fighting his corner. As we waited for Lauren to work her magic, we decided to name the little featherweight fighter.

This was one of a long line of tiny lifeless baby birds, all of whom I had called Mighty the...whatever number. I think this little one was Mighty the Fifteenth – I can't properly remember now. Teary-eyed Emma agreed it was a fitting name, and Simon nodded too. So the 15th Mighty of Greatstone (M15) was christened without him even being present.

Lauren returned to the room and told us that all she could really do was push everything back inside and seal the skin back together with surgical glue. It was a long shot, she told us, but worth a try. We were all grateful for her efforts and were all smiles as we left the vet's office. We knew our M15 was not out of the woods, but we would now do everything we normally did – and more – to hand-rear any tiny baby handed in.

We sat in the car and marvelled at our now very active and hungry new addition. Simon asked me if I knew what type of bird M15 might be, but the only clue was the pieces of red-flecked white pieces of eggshell.

'A blue tit,' I assured him with confidence. The Mightys that had come before him had been an array of garden birds from tits, sparrows, a single black bird, collar doves and even a wild parakeet. The first Mighty had been a sparrow being found in Greatstone in Kent, hence the title. Each given the name for their delicateness that soon grew into such strength, leading to their eventual release. On their release my hand-reared birds always left me with a lump in my throat due to the many perils newly fledge birds faced; my heart would always sink. After all, I was a doting parent like any other.

Once back at the centre, Emma and Simon wished me good luck with the very delicate responsibility they had entrusted to me and went back their normal life. Mighty would be one of the many newborns who needed me all day every day. This was normal life for me: an airing cupboard full of baby birds and mammals, and a guest bathroom full of the next-stage babies. My tortoise slept in the house every night and had full access to their gardens during the day, whereas Pamela the quail loved chilling on the sofa in the lounge. My life is a timer of baby feeds, dog walks, poo-picking, work, Retreat and then repeat (and trying to write this book, too).

Mighty took to his feeds like a dream. He was the tiniest of creatures, with transparent skin and a wound across his abdomen – so vulnerable yet so strong. From the start, I knew he was a gladiator. His little frame grew by the day, with eyes that could soon spot me and wings that shimmered with excitement when he knew his feed was due. As he got bigger, he joined a group of other babies, but he remained different. He never enjoyed the company of the others, but was always waiting for Dad to appear. Once fully feathered, he stood out not only because of his habit of climbing up the side of the juvenile pen when he spotted me, but because his feathers never grew over his scar. Just like the famous Zorro retained his zigzag on the side of his face, our Mighty stood proud with his belt of no feathers across his waist.

The other birds in the pen took their feeds but were happy to leave behind the human feeding them, but not Mighty. M15 would fly onto me, and sit on my head or shoulders to groom me. He was reluctant to return to his pen, taking to flying off and landing on the curtains, constantly calling and chirping as if saying '*Dad, up here, here I am! I'm not going to fly off, I'm a good boy.*' I would pretend to leave the room and Mighty would fly back onto me, trying out his distraction tactics. Sometimes my boy would try to bite my fingers as I returned him to his pen, and I'd explain to him that this was unacceptable gratitude.

My birds grew into fine young wild adolescents each day, becoming more and more ready for the wild – all except for Mighty. When it reached flight time in the aviary, he still hung on to the sides to see what Dad was up to. When the big day finally arrives and the pop holes in the flight are open, your now very independent young adult birds in their groups can take to the air. The flight remains set up as a safety zone with food until the birds are finding everything they need. Most leave and don't return; they discover that freedom was the missing component in their lives and go on to live 'free as a bird'. I was more than surprised when Mighty left us without saying goodbye, and didn't come back for the buffet of food available in the flight. There was absolutely nothing, no sign of my special boy.

The summer of 2020 arrived with its incredible heat wave. During the scorching lockdown I was resting comfortably on a sun chair in the shade with my chin on my fist after some tidying up. I was enjoying forty winks while the rest of the world was at a standstill, unable to do much else. Like a castaway, hidden all alone under my favourite cherry tree (on a beautifully comfortable wooden sun lounger kindly gifted to me by great supporters of our centre Tony and June), I snoozed the afternoon away whilst wildlife reclaimed the empty cities all over the world, from the now tourist-free canals of Venice to the villages where deer were now walking freely, whilst hunters were at home under house arrest – but the best surprise of all was about to happen.

I woke to the feeling of something on my nose. Hoping it wasn't a hornet, I opened my eyes slowly. To my amazement, sitting on top of my fist and pecking at my nose was a very healthy blue tit. I looked into his eyes and he continued to make a meal of my nose, rubbing his tiny face on my cheek. I lowered my hand slowly in an attempt to kiss the little bird. He stared back at me, and my heart missed a beat. The movement of my hand was too much for his liking, and he flew off – but not before I saw his featherless belt. He landed high up in the cherry tree, where another perfect blue tit was awaiting her mate. Emotional, I laid back. I couldn't believe my boy was hanging around somewhere. All the hard work, all the blood, sweat and tears, really did pay off. I texted Emma and Simon to tell them the good news, and they were over the moon.

After that I kept an eye out every day for my special one, but saw no sign. The months I had him, we were so very close, and that fleeting moment on my hand indicated he also remembered our very strong bond. *Will he return?* I continued to ask myself. To my amazement, there was one more short visit before he left home for good, and I experienced the dreaded realisation of 'empty nest syndrome'.

A year later, Neil and I were eating supper in the garden under the many vines and climbers – including Wisteria, Rambling Roses, Jasmine and Passion Fruit – covering our pagoda. The beautiful terrace where we eat most nights hangs full of bunches of grapes and broad vine leaves. There was usually a lot going on above us: butterflies, bees, rusty-coloured hornets, small birds and the odd grey squirrel. But today was different. From the corner of my eye, I caught sight of a flash of blue. I sat still and watched as a very confident blue tit bobbed along the green covered rafters above us. He was not bug-finding, but checking me out. As he moved along towards us, twisting and turning his neck to catch our attention he looked down straight at me, as if to say something. Neil had also noticed him.

We placed our cutlery down and watched the little fella's escapades unfold above us. He soon dropped down onto the dinner table like he owned the place and then flew down right onto my foot. The cheeky chappy grabbed the lace of my shoe and started shaking it, obviously trying to get my attention. I remained puzzled but lowered my head to greet our dinner guest. Without hesitation, he hopped onto my open hand and greeted me with a few of his unique little love-bites. At this point there was no doubting it. I knew exactly who had made a grand entrance.

Mighty the Fifteenth of Greatstone stood all grown up in the palm of my hand. A very proud father-son moment, I felt as if I was watching him on his graduation day. After a minute, Mighty took flight up into the dense green jungle canopy covering our home. I honestly think he had come to say 'Farewell, Dad'. It had been a privilege to watch this tiny marvel on his journey from shattered shell to happy adulthood – a pure Disney moment in time.

Chapter Five: The power of your voice

My viewpoint in life is always an optimistic one. I see the glass half full, half full of resources to work with rather than half empty with nothing. I pick my way through the tiniest morsels of goodwill to build the foundations of something great. I'll always congratulate the hope in any positive steps taken, rather than ruminating on what more could be done.

Humans aren't clones. There isn't a 'one-size-fits-all' method to changing the world, and many people will only adapt as laws do, remaining incapable of any kind of change until that point. You can't force change on that type of mindset, but instead can move on to the next person showing signs of an open mind.

Man's biggest challenge is not evil, but indifference. Outreach is often slow and frustrating, but I want to celebrate and encourage absolutely every step in the right direction. No matter how small, every step is a win for the animals, planet earth and your outreach skills. Every right move is a way of opening minds and challenging the wrongs we have all been fed for so long. Try not to forget that everyone had to start somewhere. You don't need to know every fact and figure on your subject. You just need to know your audience. Are the people in front of you interested in their health, saving the planet, being kind to animals, eating good food, going out and partying, making money? Every angle will be a way in to talk about kindness.

One important area which benefits animals, but is rarely promoted, is the power of your voice within your own circle – sometimes from your own sofa. We all have our own spectators, whether they be digital (through gaming or social media), or through physical means like meet-ups with friends and family, in your place of work, clubs you attend or even spotting somebody hovering over a product in the supermarket. It can be as simple as explaining to the person hovering over the ready-meals: 'I recently had that plant-based dish and it was out of this world. Go on, you won't be disappointed.'

You don't need to make time for this kind of outreach. Leading by example is a powerful way of exciting and educating your own listeners. You don't want people turning off, disengaging or unfollowing your social media. Stay fresh and engaging, celebrating facts and figures with a *'can you believe it?'* attitude, showing how much you enjoy learning and how eager you are to be a better person – a kind of custodian of our planet and its earth-sharers. Gandhi once said 'You can never lose a moral argument'. Your voice and every word that comes out of your mouth can be a make-or-break statement of justice for animals, a zero or hero moment. What more encouragement do you need? Give it your best shot, and think of it as a teacher and pupil scenario. Now, let's start teaching.

One of my favourite forms of outreach is calling into radio stations on any topic and turning the discussion to the pressing animal issue of our time. For instance, when the famous shot of the poor polar bear on a melting iceberg sparked international conversation about global warming – with absolutely no mention of animal agriculture – I came in with my list of did-you-knows. With every twist and turn in the interviewer's arrogance, I mentioned how kind and gentle farm animals are, the atrocious way they're treated, and the environmental disaster modern farming methods are causing, plus the damage caused to our health, including the spread of global pandemics, until the host called time and cut me off.

Another time I decided to use my voice and be an advocate for animals was at a slaughterhouse in London. I turned up expecting to be able to reason with those queuing to choose their victim and end the little creature's life.I began explaining that being at this kind of establishment showed no kindness, compassion or respect to non-human animals, and that there are kinder routes to take. I was mid-debate, with every casebook scenario in defence of harming the gentlest of animals being thrown at me, when something unexpected happened.

A sprightly red hen rushed out of the slaughterhouse door, flapping and clucking in terror, and then shot across the pavements and into the crowd. The slender little red chicken was determined to live and dodged in and out of the crowd's feet and shopping bags. Mesmerised by her break for freedom, I realised my debate was futile. If any good was going to come of today, I had to leave and catch the clever girl and then get her out of here. Before I could make my dash to save her the slaughterhouse emptied of workers dressed in white bloodstained overalls and wearing white wellies blooded by the already fallen. They rushed out after the chicken to drag her back into their hellhole.

Many humans seem to be under illusions that the slaughterhouse system is a sort of holiday camp for animals, complete with lasting friendships and happy memories, before they willingly gift us their body parts nicely wrapped in cellophane. This couldn't be further from the truth, but there's no time to explain – I've got a chicken to save.

Out came the slaughter team with their meat cleavers, army knives and broomsticks, a real group of insurgents like the villains in a Rambo movie. Surely not all of this for one escaped bird? It felt like a real East London gangland meet, and an old fashion Reggie and Ronnie Cray style fight was just about to break out. The other mobster, however, was not one of the infamous Richardsons (rival gangland family to The Crays) but a lone worn out egg layer, a tiny bird who broke out, a chicken on the loose. The irony of a fugitive 'food animal' on the run is that almost everyone wants her to survive, to get away and escape death and then live out her days in the paradise of an animal sanctuary. How much easier would it be to simply not pay for the products that support such industries?

The tiny little lady ducked and dived and made her way through the streets of shoppers. All she needed was a miracle that would save her. She was one of the only creatures with no protection under UK law, in the way that she lived or died – but now she had her miracle at last, and that was me. I shoved people out of the way to keep up with her, but she was too fast. I scrambled after Miss Run-Away on all fours, but she was still ahead of me. She knew I was after her and moved swiftly, zigzagging out of arm's reach each time I got within a feather of catching her. To her, all humans were the same: blood junkies. She had no reason to think I was any different. Within second she outsmarted me and disappeared yet again. I was her only ally – if only I had a way to explain this to her.

'She's behind the bins!' a woman's voice shouted. Forgetting I was not the only one after our Speedy Gonzales, I crawled around the back of the multiple wire storage cages filled with discarded cardboard and plastic. I lay on the floor and reached right to the back of the rubbish to feel the feathered wreck's heart beating through her tiny frame. As I pulled her out from the safety of the bins, her terrified amber eyes stared into mine in fear. I heard voices in the crowd behind me, but never expected it to be the slaughter workers in full pursuit of such a tiny bird. In financial terms, she was virtually worthless – yet I was completely outnumbered, and the workers' resentment for me was already at an all-time high thanks to my peaceful outreach earlier. To them, I had declared an all-out war without even knowing it.

Our girl may have been behind enemy lines but now there were two of us. The workers, all brandishing their weapons, were determined to finish off my new partner in crime (and me too, judging by the looks on their nasty faces). It wasn't a case of 'handbags at dawn'. I had nothing to protect us...or so I thought.

In this fight-or-flight scenario, my fighting instincts took hold. I had two choices: keep running with Birdie, or hand her over to a fate worse than death. I was never going to hand her over, of course – over my dead body. No animal deserved even to witness those atrocities. Within a second, I was gone.

Like Shergar, the world's fastest racehorse, my long legs bolted. I fled the packed roads just behind London's famous Commercial Street, once the feared stomping ground of Jack the Ripper, whose own cruelty was now a distant memory marked by local history tours. With Miss Run-Away securely under wraps, I ran for both of our lives, with no idea where I was going as I tried desperately to remember which lane led to which street.

The murder squad was after me. Even if I made it to Aldgate East railway station, who was to say I'd be safe there? Exhausted, I pushed myself on to the Commercial Road, running down the street completely breathless and out of ideas. Then, I saw a lifeline. My heart pounding through my chest, the leg muscles I'd forgotten I had screaming for a rest, I seized my opportunity for the great escape. A slow-moving council truck collecting the cardboard left out by market traders was just pulling out onto the main road. I had no other choice but to make one last sprint and grab the tailgate of my accidental chariot.

The truck accelerated at a speed no slaughter-man could even wish to catch, my trainers dragging along the tarmac at roughly 30 miles per hour. I manoeuvred to twist my neck and head to see the death crew starting to fade into the distance surrounded by Sunday shoppers. With their waves of angry fists and shouts of *'You won't get away with it!'*, I gripped the truck tightly and counted my lucky blessings. The council worker who had unknowingly become my getaway driver cruised along happily, his stowaways hanging off the back. A moped rider passing me looked on with bewilderment on his face. It must have crossed his mind that there are surely easier ways of getting around London. At last, I'd found the lucky break I needed to put me ahead of London's real villains.

Unable to pull myself fully onto the back of the truck, I hung on for several minutes until a red light slowed my obliging chariot to a halt. In a rather undignified style, I dropped off the back of the truck, watched by the gobsmacked passenger in the car behind me as I rearranged my little feathered friend who now sat comfortably inside my jacket. With Aldgate East station on my right, I rushed in and boarded the very first train. Birdie seemed happy and settled, tucked away inside the sanctuary of my layers.

Miss Run-Away was later christened Zola after Zola Bud, the South African long-distance runner who was famous for competing barefoot. Our Zola so deserved a gold medal that day, not only for outsmarting her captors but for her legendary obstacle race through the streets of London.

Like Shergar the racehorse Zola had to disappear, and I only hope the world-famous racehorse lived his life in exile like our very special little fugitive did. Rolling hills and green meadows, a snug house with deep straw, surrounded by our displaced chicken friends, is now life for Zola, the one who got away.

Chapter Six: Spy cops

Campaigning for animal rights has always seemed the logical choice for me. Animals have an unbelievable lack of justice on their side, even today. Everyone knows that if you kick a child, puppy, lamb, piglet or a calf they will experience pain, and the harder you kick, the more damage you will cause. They're only babies, after all. Yet through the eyes of the law, each baby is awarded a different level of protection.

Why would anyone want to harm an animal? And why should there be laws that only protect certain animals? The answer is simply that we wish to use and abuse certain animals, and not others. (Though there are some exceptions to this – for example, the government might arbitrarily justify harming cats and dogs in cruel and unreliable laboratory experiments.)

It's well known that people who harm animals often move on rapidly to harming other humans. It's a fact we can't get away from – harmers are harmers. Research has revealed that twenty-five percent of aggressive inmates had committed multiple acts of animal abuse as children. Forty-five percent of school shooters had histories of alleged animal cruelty and twenty-one percent of serial murderers admitted to childhood animal abuse. This should be enough to turn us all away from animal abuse, but does it?

Many well-intentioned people campaign for animal welfare, which is the complete opposite to what animal rights activists campaign for. Those concerned with welfare issues – bigger cages, enriched environments, and shorter journeys to slaughter, for example – don't accept the argument for animal rights. Seeing this most important point would undermine their own agenda. The welfare argument is completely debunked by the animal rights one. In short, welfarists wants to have their cake (and not a cruelty-free one at that) and eat it too.

Campaigning for animal rights could see you on the wrong side of the law. You could be arrested or even sent to prison for no reason other than standing up for kindness and compassion, and many laws have been brought in to hinder the activities of campaigners. These laws have seen ordinary, kind people sent to prison for running successful campaigns to close down animal harming establishments. Animal rights campaigners have dismantled the anti-animal myths surrounding fox hunting, exposing the use of 'bagged foxes' – foxes bred in artificial sets and then hunted for sport – proving that it's not 'pest control', but comes from pure bloodlust. Covert cameras have caught live foxhounds being thrown into the incinerator at hunt kennels, and hunt horses being shot when they are no longer able to hunt.

There was also the badger cull – the government culling of a protected species due to misinformation surrounding the spread of Bovine TB. Sadly, many cattle who appear to test positive for Bovine TB are actually found to be negative at their autopsy. Even if, hypothetically speaking, badgers were responsible for the spread of Bovine TB, then the poisoning, trapping and shooting of these creatures would simply cause those living in sets to scatter in search of a safer place to live – further contributing to the spread of the disease. It would be far more reliable, and much kinder, to vaccinate and tag the badgers instead, to collect accurate data. It's also interesting to consider whether badgers are the only mammal to roam the countryside, potentially spreading TB. Once again, animal rights campaigners have highlighted the hypocrisy, exposing the real reason for the extermination of one of our most iconic wildlife creatures. Other exposes have shed light on the cruelty of the race horse industry, greyhound racing, laboratory testing, puppy farms, factory farms, seal pup slaughter, Seaworld, slaughterhouse torture...the list goes on and on.

In my many years of campaigning, attending rallies to end the fur trade, World Day for Animals and many others, I've met some amazing people. These are people who share the same common ground, wanting to make a difference for animals. Over the years we have formed instant friendships which are still alive today. Being young and naïve, I always took people at face value, never expecting there to be an ulterior motive. People like fellow activist Christine.

Christine was a woman in her late thirties. She was casually dressed, with nicely kept hair, and she was keenly interested in getting involved. I thought she was great – a thinker and a planner, and somebody with a lot to give – and an immediate friendship formed. Within no time at all, Christine was at every demo, local or national, giving anyone a lift or a listening ear. Everyone knew Christine and Christine knew everyone. She became a driver and organiser and very quickly sat at every strategic planning meeting.

As mates do, Christine and I spent a lot of time together. I was sure she was going to score great goals in animal rights. She was a very capable person – a skilled cook and driver, and somebody I loved being with. I often visited her London flat where we ate delicious curries and imaginative salads; she was a natural when it came to creating delicious foods. Her home was so sparse and tidy, a reflection of her no-nonsense character – or so I thought. There were no personal nick-nacks, no photos, plants or books. Being a hoarder, I was intrigued by her discipline. I never once suspected what the whisperers had started to say.

There was never a cup in the sink or a wet towel left on the floor. Christine never ran out of loo roll or soya milk, unlike the rest of us struggling to keep everything going. She never mentioned any financial issues. She told us she worked as a courier, hence her small immaculate van. Christine never missed a meeting or a meet up, everything from weddings, pub drinks, curry nights, house parties to demonstrations; our new uncomplicated friend would be there from start to finish. Christine knew where I worked and lived; in fact, she knew where all her new friends lived and worked and shared everything in our lives as mates do.

Somebody once jokingly mentioned to me, in passing, that Christine *could* be an undercover police officer, with all of us under her surveillance: 'Loose lips sink ships.' She had arrived from nowhere, and had joined the local animal rights meeting with no traceable history. She

43

allowed us to believe that she was the private type, so never needed to mention any other friends or family. Everyone loved Christine, and we could not see the blatantly obvious plainclothes copper for the trees. Before we knew it we were all BFFs (best friends forever), and Christine even got herself an animal rights campaigner for a boyfriend. Our friendships strengthened, and Christine became more and more involved in our campaigning. She became privy to private planning meetings as we discussed what was next on our agenda, how we could progress our work helping animals. She was now a regular fixture at any high-profile event. The key to the success of many animal rights campaigns, including the closure of many animal hell-holes, was surprise. Getting to the location long before the police, so that we could lock onto our target and occupy strategic buildings, was paramount in our bid to further the cause.

As quickly as Christine came into our lives, she disappeared. After five years, she left us to pursue what she told us were personal issues – gone, just like that. Activists began to look deeper into the lives of those who turned up with no commitments.

Next in the mix of activist friends was a guy called Matt Rayner, more commonly known as Chiswick. Chiswick was a similar age to Christine and oddly enough was another courier with a van. An uncomplicated friend who seemed to appear from nowhere but knew everyone. Matt lived in a sparse bedsit in Woodford London. His room consisted of double bed with one limp pillow and drab duvet set, a single wardrobe and a chest of drawers with only a soap bag stored on top. He had a fold-out kitchen table with two chairs, and his flat was full of newspapers and magazines. Nothing in his home painted a picture of him. Most ordinary people would have thought this was a regular bachelor pad, untidy and cheap. Matt fitted in well and even went on dates with female activists.

One of our friends and activist Soraya Wasenius remembers Chiswick and her date well. Matt flirted with her during our monthly London Animal Action meetings and soon built up the courage to ask her out. This was all evidence-gathering of people who the police thought were leaders in the movement. He took her address and made a date to pick her up from home. Soraya and Matt drove to Brighton and during the journey he asked her mundane questions, but when he was questioned in return he responded with only 'yes' or 'no' answers. The date was boring, and Matt appeared monosyllabic and lacking in personality, if not a little cagey.

Soraya had absolutely no suspicion that Matt was yet another undercover cop walking among us. The date was a flop with the final insult coming from Chiswick asking to split the bill (the Metropolitan Police were probably a little tight with their expenses back then). Matt dropped Soraya home after the long drive back and tried for a kiss. Soraya, double buffing with a kind wave, quickly exited the van and said her goodnights till next time, which there would never be.

Each spy cop was assigned a period of time to invade our lives and extract whatever they could find. The timescale of their fake existence was usually up to five years and then they would disappear. An 'emergency' or 'once-in-a-lifetime job offer' would immediately take them away. Far away worlds like Argentina, Australia and even Papa New Guinea were mentioned as their new homeland. It's hard to pop around to see an old mate who's now living ten thousand miles away. A pattern was emerging, and when these individuals needed to return to their day job we'd never hear from them again.

Spy cops overstepped the mark in every area. Their

fictional identities illegally took on the names of deceased children, and they intruded into our personal lives and relationships. They entered our homes by deception, and some even fathered children with activists. A mammoth public inquiry later took place, along with a landmark report, finding that the undercover department was not justified and should have been closed down, and compensation was paid to activists. This gave some closure to the dishonest behaviour, but it left many questions unanswered. Matt Rayner disappeared without another mention until the inquiry, although his whereabouts remain unknown.

Christine Green left the Met after this period and went public with an apology in the *Guardian* newspaper to the activists she claimed became friends. She remains vegan and interested in animal rights issues. The efforts put into policing and gathering evidence of animal rights activists shows how effective our campaigns have been in waking up the public to the plight of animals. The moral of this story is the power of kindness; even Metropolitan Police special branch officers could be converted to doing the right thing and turn their backs on cruelty, and live a kinder life.

Chapter Seven:
June and the giant peach

There are so many things we can all do to help animals. Things that don't cost us money at all, but only require time. Kind choices when shopping and eating make an impact on animals, and can influence your audience. 'Humane slaughter' and 'free range' are pure myths, scams which people continue to believe and pay for. They are marketing terms which make us feel happy, but have no positive impact on the animals. It doesn't matter whether an animal is free range, organic, corn- or grass- fed – they all end up at the same slaughterhouse, not the Holiday Inn, the insult to injury being that you funded it.

Supporters have come up with all sorts of great ways of helping the residents at The Retreat. Sue at *The County Chronicle* magazine runs a free full-page article for The Retreat every month, Steve and Shelia Bunny arranged a valentine's dance once a year with live music and the ticket sales from the great night supported our residents. Some of our residents appear on the packets of some products of The Green Kitchen Cafe Brighton, with funds from each sale helping us, and Abbie of MMXNSON Tattoos kindly does flash days in support of our work. Abbie is an influencer on social media. Then there's Angela of Sevenoaks Animal Feeds in Kent who supplies dog food free of charge to our darling canine residents on medication. Sara Starkey and Chris Fosbury giving their time every week to volunteer in our cruelty-free cafe. Nikki and Zoe Smith volunteer with us weekly, and take home all our orphaned ducklings each year to rear them to adulthood, including swimming lessons in their bathtub. People have found so many incredible ways to support us.

Doing transport runs for animal rescue can be a great way of getting involved. If you can't use the animal rescue vehicle, most rescues will cover the costs of your fuel. These transport runs can be to pick up and drop off animals, take them to the vet, or to pick up supplies. There's Andrea Charlewood who does weekly feed collections and travels the four-hour round trip to us with her truck full of crucial everyday staples. Regan and Jerry of Next Chapter Animal Rescue stockpile massive amounts of food and other animal related goodies for us at their home in Camberley. Rescue centres are busy places and things need collecting all the time, from veterinary medicines, injured wildlife, strays and even fresh fruit and vegetables. There's a job for everyone and for all ages and abilities.

At The Retreat we were lucky to be offered all the unsold fruit and veg from Spitalfields Market East London. We did the shout out for help and two wonderful helpers offered to go and collect. Ellie and June were in their sixties when they came aboard to ferry the fresh produce from London to Kent. Off they would go on the three-hour round trip in June's faithful Ford Mondeo. The market was full of delicious mountains of fresh unsold goodies. It was like winning the lotto but being paid in juicy ripe fruit currency. Everything from all corners of the earth including the most exotic pieces of fruit like Breadfruit and the most odd-looking vegetables ever. June and Ellie would pack the car full of the most colourful foods imaginable. Melons and cauliflowers were rolled under the driver and passenger seats and on the back seats they stacked coconuts, apples, cabbages, potatoes, starfruit, mangos, pomegranates, bananas, pineapples, lychees and kiwi fruit layered to the ceiling. No more than a tiny chilli would now fit. The girls would drive back with single pieces of fruit packed around the headrests, creating a kind of Carmen Miranda fruit crash helmet with the last of the bunches of grapes, an odd strawberry or handful of cherries topped with a lone banana. Sometimes a rare find like a giant peach would travel home on a lap, saved for Magic or Tierra, two of the pigs who were first in line for their treats having learned the sound of June's car.

The mouth-watering five-star banquet would be sorted into buckets to give everyone a vibrant and vitamin-packed lunch. June and Ellie knew all our residents, and knew each individual's favourite fresh treat. On days where market days coincided with June's babysitting duties for her beautiful granddaughter, Anna, the baby would be packed into the car, too. The best market finds of the day would be packed around the baby's car seat, framing Anna in fruit and veg. A ripe, organic fair-trade banana would be handed to the well-behaved youngster, along with some broccoli for her amusement, or some lunch for her obliging behaviour. These epic road trips of vegetable savage by The Retreat's very own Thelma and Louise (or Hinge and Bracket) actually made Anna a real-life cabbage patch doll.

A few years on and The Retreat received a donation of a Ford Transit van, which became June's new deluxe fruit truck. Due to the girls' eagerness to bring home every last piece of unwanted fruit and veg the van had a taped line around the inside to prevent the vehicle being overloaded with fruity treasures. This meant that under the seats across the dashboard and occasionally in the glove-compartment baby carrots, mustard and cress or water-chestnuts could be found hidden away. They were like vegetable smugglers and no small void escaped their dutiful eye.

Both June and Ellie were destined to make the world a better place and would spend their time if not at the market, trapping and neutering feral cats around Kent and London. I remember a wonderful tale of their kindness when out collecting for Save The Children in Bromley. They knocked on a door canvassing for donations and was met with a grumpy woman many years their junior.

'Who are you collecting for?' the woman asked, noticing the information packs June was holding. 'It better not be for animals.'

'No, it's for Save the Children,' June replied softly. The woman graciously handed her fifty pence from her cardigan pocket. June then asked the woman why she didn't want to support animals, and was taken aback by her mean-spirited answer.'

'Those people are just trouble makers, only caring about animals,' she answered.

'Ellie and I are "animal people",' June explained, in her kind an unpatronising voice, 'and out of the whole population of Bromley, no one else was available to collect for Save the Children, just two little old ladies who also care enough about animal suffering to do something about it. Maybe you would like to join us with the next Save the Children collection?'

'No,' snapped the Scrooge of Bromley. 'I'm far too old to walk the streets.'

Kindness is not an orange with separate segments you can pick and choose to care about. Kindness is a loving and protecting feeling, that fits all.

Chapter Eight:
The Battle of Trafalgar

In 2001, London's Trafalgar Square's last pigeon-seed seller agreed in court to stop selling bird-seed to the hundreds of thousands of tourists who came every year hoping for a pigeon to land on their head or hand held out with the lucky seed. The seed seller took his cash settlement and deserted the two famous flocks of approximately 4000 Trafalgar Square pigeons that for generations got the visitors' kind gifts every day.

The man behind this hideously cruel and thoughtless decision was Ken Livingstone, who was mayor of London at the time. 'Red Ken' unintelligently and absurdly dubbed pigeons 'rats with wings', whilst most people are educated enough to know the difference between bird and mammals. Mr Livingstone delighted in the demonising of the iconic landmark bird, and loved the coverage it got him. How stupid and short-sighted – after all, most historic cities have their own flock of much-loved pigeons adorning iconic places like St Mark's Square in Venice, or Central Park in New York. London's very own pigeon hater may have thought he'd won the Battle of Trafalgar, but whilst the wars of his private life flooded the tabloids with headlines about his violence and lies, the public were now starting to see the true nature of the man they'd voted into power.

From 1943 to 1949, thirty-two pigeons were awarded the Dickin Medal to acknowledge actions of gallantry and devotion during the Second World War and subsequent conflicts. The Dickin Medal is a bronze medallion, bearing the words 'For Gallantry'. It wasn't just pigeons who were awarded it, but also eighteen dogs, three horses and a ship's cat. This gallantry and devotion to duty while serving (although the animals had no choice in the matter) in military conflict meant nothing to Red Ken. But behind the scenes, an army of animal advocates were planning their strategies to save the Trafalgar Square pigeons from starvation.

A feeding rota was put into place, so the birds wouldn't wake up to no breakfast. The resident flocks – generation after generation of birds who'd never left the square – would have been doomed without the dedication of a small group of devoted animal activists. A small handful of people of all ages refused to be discouraged by Mr Livingstone's army of doormats who tried to implement cruel bylaws to harm the pigeons. While London's police force, who I'm sure had more worthy crimes to deal with, enforced the absurd law against feeding the birds, the Pigeon Protection Party came up with genius ideas like pull-along shopping trolleys, or suitcases with holes cut in the bottom to discreetly deposit seed across the square for the hungry birds. With minders placed on the battle ground to stop any feeding, more ingenious ideas were needed.

Some feeders took to wearing disguises while others distracted the minders with woes of lost children and minor first-aid issues, as their subordinates deposited as much seed as possible under the benches. Soon, it became apparent that the vast amounts of seed required to maintain the birds would be best dropped at night under the cover of darkness. Mr Livingstone seemed to have an unlimited budget to deal with the pigeon-feeding troops, while the people of London needed so much. Unbeknown to the volunteers back then, this was to last sixteen years, until the last of the flocks eventually moved out of the square.

Our turn to feed and collect the poorly and sad pigeons were on a Thursday night. 120 kilos of bird seed were purchased during the day and stacked into Pee-Pee (Pigeon Peugeot), our very own allocated pigeon feeding car. Then each sack of seed was decanted into bag-for-life shopping carriers – 'La Birdie luggage'. Not quite up to Louis Vuitton standards, but these smaller and more discreet bags did the job. They enabled us to reach the drop-off point without being hijacked or arrested by the Boys in Blue.

Our four covert drop-off points were behind The National Gallery inside the tree gates, Whitehall Gardens opposite Embankment Station and parallel with the River Thames (ironically home to the statues of heroes from bygone battles who actually understood the importance of our now outcast once well decorated feathered hero),

Charlton House Terrace under the bins, and along the grassy areas adjacent to The Royal Mail. Even at well past 11pm, some birds would fly down to eat what they could, while others waited until the first light, before the road cleaners could clear away any remaining seed.

My team would usually eat pizza first somewhere around Charing Cross, waiting for the hordes of people to lessen. It was my love for all creatures (especially the underdog) that made me find the energy for every Thursday night pigeon feed after an exhausting week of work and rescue. The eight o'clock drive from Kent to central London was never a chore and I drove it to ensure those birds were never disappointed. During the early days I would always find a few birds needing some extra TLC and we brought them home and nursed them back to health in our kitchen. The flocks that call The Retreat home now are still many of the original Trafalgar Square Pigeons.

One extremely funny feeding situation was when a friend and I were discreetly dropping the seed off to one of our feeding points when an accusing voice came from behind me, asking what I was up to. Turning around, I discovered two dazzling Drag Queens, both with a hand on one hip and a cigarette in the other hand. They were more real-life ugly sisters than Cinderella dressed up for the ball; it may have been midnight, but they wanted answers. With no glass slipper, golden carriage, footmen or white horses, they still seemed to own the night. One was dressed completely in green, the other all in dark red, looking a real treat (or maybe more of a Halloween trick). With their newly fixed bouffant hairstyles like the great Dusty Springfield was their stylist, and they wore the highest of heels like mini stepladders.

I stepped forward to greet them with a 'Good evening ladies, how are you? You're both looking fabulous tonight…now let me explain just what we're up to…' I introduced us both and, after giving a short history lesson on the bird residents of Trafalgar Square, Miss Emerald interrupted me.

'You keep saying birds,' she cut in. 'They're not birds. Parrots and eagles are birds – *they're* pigeons.' With her sidekick Miss Ruby nodding in agreement, I caught sight of something that fascinated me. Miss Emerald was wearing earrings with green cucumbers hanging off the ring, and a necklace of interlinked cucumbers too. Miss Ruby also had cherries adorning her earrings and necklace, the detail beyond intricate. I wondered if other small symbols of veganism could be found on their persons. Surely they should have been dripping in their namesake rubies and emeralds? I thought they'd missed a trick with their own personal fashion statement.

I didn't dare ask the symbolism of their accessories, fearing a shocking tale of crimes against vegetables could be unleashed. I reined in my imagination, reasoning that I should focus on explaining exactly what makes a bird a bird.

'Now ladies,' I said cheerfully, 'please think for a minute what makes a bird a bird.' Immediately, I was met with the usual nonsense.

'They lay eggs,' Miss Emerald said self-righteously, pulling out a nail file to tend to her perfectly polished bright-green nails.

'No,' I replied, 'because insects, reptiles, fish and even the duck-billed platypus – a mammal – lay eggs too.' I laughed enthusiastically, having stated this a million times before.

It was Miss Ruby's turn. 'They fly,' she smirked, with a triumphant look at Miss E.

'Flying fish, flying squirrels and of course bats that fly are mammals too,' I said, beaming from ear to ear, 'and

54

remember there's also flightless birds like the now-extinct Dodo, the ostrich and the emu too.' I proudly sealed the deal with my words of wisdom. Puzzled, the two drag queens looked at each other and sighed in disappointment. Their expressions made it clear to me that they had no time for my game of Trivial Pursuit, and they were obviously poor losers. They fiddled in their colour-coordinated shoulder bags for anything to distract from my biology lesson. They'd had enough and were ready to move on, but I exclaimed the answer to my question in an excited bid to rebuild their interest.

'Feathers!' I declared, more loudly and theatrically than ever, which I guessed was what was needed. 'Feathers are what makes a bird a bird. It's plain and simple, just feathers. Can either of you think of anything that's not a bird that has feathers?' Miss Emerald, the more upfront of the precious stones, lit another cigarette, cool as a cucumber.

'A feather duster,' she muttered under her breath. *Touché*. In disbelief, I doubled over with laughter and uncontrollable giggles from the depths of my belly anchored me.

'A feather duster!' I cried. It was at this point that our next two interested bystanders walked over to investigate the burst of laughter. Their intrigue at the disturbance on the deserted backstreet got the better of them, and they came to investigate what was going on.

Our two new pupils for tonight's pigeon class were two suits – young banker types, suited and booted – on their way to the station after a night celebrating some big wins at work. Samuel and Matthew introduced themselves and asked what was so funny to create such a performance. Samuel's puzzled face starred down at the tree grates filled to the brim with birdseed. Matthew continued with his questioning, quizzing the girls on their involvement in tonight's street entertainment before turning to me, having been pointed my way by the girls. A million questions followed, and although I was interested by *their* interest, I had other areas to drop the food before the night was out...

Noticing the time, the suits realised they'd missed their last train home and would need to grab a taxi. I asked where they lived, in case I could help, and they told me they were from South London. Without hesitation, I negotiated a deal. I proposed that I'd give them a ride home on one condition: that they helped me with the last of the feeding. At this point, everyone agreed to join me and my feeding companion to ensure the pigeons of London did not go hungry.

At this rate we could have done the conga around London and been less conspicuous. How easy was it to get 'ordinary' people to action for animals in need. Team Pigeon was very much ready to be launched. With such panache, Miss E and Miss R climbed into the back seat, arranging themselves into a more ladylike and comfortable position before making way for our other passengers. There was one seat for the two suits to fit into, so I called to the girls to squeeze up and make room. Emerald warned them that Miss Ruby was a man-eater at best, a black widow at worse – *Same difference,* I thought.

'So watch where you sit, and behave yourself!' Miss Emerald proclaimed. The two party boys at heart then burst into song, singing the chorus of Hall and Oates's 'Man Eater', belting the lyrics: '*Watch out boy she'll chew you up, Oh here she comes, she's a man eater...*' We all sang along, enjoying the uplifting atmosphere of the Pigeon Peugeot. We drove to our drop-offs and each new recruit emptied their contraband in the hide-out for the early morning pigeon; in this case the early bird didn't get the worm, but kilos of good quality seed.

Tonight's feeders didn't realise just how important they were, with each one of them based in Central London for part of a day or night each day of the week. Samuel and Matthew both started work early in the morning, coming into Charing Cross Station, while our ladies both worked the night. With a few short lessons in what to do if they found a poorly or baby pigeon, they became first aiders and life savers. A cotton tote bag could be folded to the size of a handkerchief and kept in any sized bag or jacket. These bags are a fantastic portable pigeon carrier and will keep your bird comfortable and calm until you can get help.

I dropped the ladies off to their destination in Soho just outside Madame Jojo's and they disappeared up a staircase with just a discreet wave, but not before we'd exchanged contact details and they had agreed wholeheartedly to help any pigeon in distress. I dropped the last of our new recruits off at their house share in Woolwich, and they too promised their devotion to duty. Since we first met, I've called them into action three times over the years to urgent London rescues, and they've never failed the birds.

With or without a companion, I went out whatever the weather, always hoping to see a happy little face pecking the seed. I also never failed to take carrier bags of sandwiches, fruit, biscuits, bottled water and nuts for London's homeless humans too.

Another highlight of my pigeon feeding shift was to see the tiny jet-black mice that lived inside the tiles on the back of The National Gallery come out with their young to collect seed too. Literally hundreds of these busy family-oriented creatures made it to our free banquet every time.

My great friend and pigeon feeder coordinator PJ seem to be able to remain below the police and authorities' radar and never attract a crowd, but for me it was always different. City police, private security, drunks and the odd wannabe yob would try to sabotage my efforts.

'We don't sweat the small stuff,' I would remind myself, recalling the famous mantra of Violet, my dog-rescuer friend in Istanbul. I always talked my way out of being arrested, knowing that the pigeons getting their 'Ready Brek' was the only thing that mattered. Being detailed by the powers that be did sometimes mean a bag or two of seed was confiscated, but there were always plenty more hidden a road away in my incognito pidg-mobile. The police would threaten arrest, fines, court appearances, ASBOs, even jail, but I always assured them that, if not me, someone else would be back tomorrow night. Pigeons really did have friends – and some determined ones at that.

On a drive home from an uneventful pigeon feed, I spotted a big hairy dog on the loose. I pursued him up and down some back streets, until he arrived at a very dark block of apartments with one ground floor light on. The dog, now calm, sat staring at the blue door with the light on. Even though it was midnight, I went to knock on the door – after all, the dog seemed to know he was home. In my 'I can talk animal' voice (in this case, dog), I spoke to the faithful canine.

'Is this your house? Do you live here?' The wag of the dog's tail was all I needed to bang loudly with my knuckles. An uninterested man opened the door, completely blanking me as the dog ran in, the door slamming closed behind them. Without a thank you from the man or the dog, I strolled back to the car with Scarlet and two other helpers, all of whom just needed their beds at this point. We were all pizza-d and pigeon-ed out.

'Don't worry,' I said. 'We'll be home in an hour at the

latest; the roads are empty.' We took our seats in the car and took off. Before long, we were back on the main Camberwell New Road in South London. Scarlet, my front-seat passenger, was already asleep, and both the helpers in the back were away with the fairies too. I was more than happy listening to the late-night call-in show on the radio, where other insomniacs shared what they were up to in the early hours. Tales of odd drinks and love letters, a few amateur vampires and werewolves, were the oddest of the night's twilight callers. No story was quite as eccentric as ours, but we didn't have the energy to call up and plead for the poor pigeons' plight tonight.

I relaxed into driver mode – after all, what else could happen tonight? Just then, the night bus in front of me swerved on to the other side of the road to avoid hitting something. In that split second, all I could do was hit the breaks in an emergency stop, abruptly waking up my passengers. The bus carried on its journey, leaving a young woman standing in the middle of the road, right in front of our car.

Staring at us, the woman mouthed the words: 'Help me, please.' She was in her mid-twenties, with wild unkempt hair and make-up running down her face, leaving black tracks all the way down to her chin. An assortment of numerous gold hoops were in her ears, and each nostril had a gold ring or two. She also wore several gold necklaces of various lengths, with a multitude of objects hanging off them, and her fingers and thumbs were covered with rings of different designs, building up her digits like knuckle-dusters. She wore very little clothing: an ill-fitting pink boob-tube, a denim mini skirt and a pair of black polished heeled knee-high boots. Thinking about it, she could have made a good zombie character in a late-night horror, but this was no time for the imagination to run wild. I jumped out of the car, leaving the engine running and the door wide open. I was followed by the evening's pigeon rescue squad to tackle what looked like our next problem.

Cathy Collins was a local 'working girl', and was feeling 'the strain of the game,' as she put it. Life wasn't going her way, and with so many personal demons she could see no way out of this brutal maze, no way of making it through a day without her addictions. Cathy cried and begged us to take her home with us, to help her escape her living nightmare. She declared her undying love for each of us and offered her services to cook, clean and look after animals if we found it in our hearts to just give her a chance.

The answer was always going to have to be no. It wasn't because we didn't have room, or we didn't care – but there was one huge issue we couldn't ignore. It was the early hours of Friday morning, and in a few hours we would all need to get ready for work. All of us except one person: Neil. Neil, my loyal and supportive husband, had Friday and only Friday off. He could cope with any number of animals, regardless of their condition, but a suicidal woman of the night was not one of his top ten things to deal with on his day off. I explained to the team that it just couldn't happen, and that we'd need to find another way to help Cathy. We couldn't leave her behind, she was too delicate. She'd been determined to throw herself under the wheels of the bus; it was the driver's quick reaction, followed by the distraction of Team Pigeon, that kept her mind off ending it all. We all climbed back into the safety of the Pigeon Peugeot and belted back up before we considered our next steps.

'Whatever happens, team, we can't do this to Neil,' I reiterated. I offered to pay for a night in a hotel for Cathy to sleep off the drugs and drink, but her answer was a hard no. Plan B was to drive to the Samaritans for professional help. So, I drove to the Samaritans building in New Cross, and asked for help via the intercom. I was told it was against company policy to leave the building, and that if I needed to get help for Cathy, she would have to ask for it herself.

Plan C – would the police help? No.

We had no plan D, but during our drive to find help for Cathy she told the team where her parents were living. It turned out that she actually still lived with them. It was now 3am, and we all needed our beds. In true rescue mission style, we were not going to give up. Cathy's parents' address led us to a vast council estate around the back of Peckham station. The few lights in the windows across the block made us yearn for our beds even more. Almost the whole of London was sleeping, apart from us. I pressed the door number on the electronic keypad and awaited the answer.

Once the door had buzzed loudly three times, a very awake voice answered 'Yeah?'

'I'm looking for the parents of Cathy please,' I replied. 'I'm standing here with her. She's not in a good way and really needs help.'

The voice at the other end sighed. 'Not again. You'll need to take her to her boyfriend's place.'

'Really?' I answered back, confused. I asked Cathy if she knew the directions to her partner's home and she nodded rather coyly.

Back in the car and feeling dejected, we drove a few roads to the destination Cathy had given us. Again, I pressed the door number on the electric buzzer of another vast sleeping council estate. This time, Cathy answered the sleepy voice at the other end: 'It's me.' (I was tempted to burst into song with 'Heathcliff, it's me, Cathy, I've come home,' quoting the epic lyrics from Kate Bush's 'Wuthering Heights'.) Cathy's knight in shining armour (or Cyclops in Bart Simpson pyjamas) opened the heavy steel door. Before I could say 'good evening', 'good morning', or request an explanation of the unimaginable events that had led to us standing here at 3am, Cathy walked into the large concrete hallway and the mythical beast standing over her closed the door.

Just like with the dog on the run earlier, there was no acknowledgement of gratitude for Team Pigeon's time or help. Our efforts, enthusiasm and energy were absolutely the same for rescuing animals and people, never compromising. Whoever needed us we would do our best for and with whatever we had.

Now safely home and my devoted team of helpers already sound asleep tucked up in bed, with a smile on my face knowing pigeons, dog and Cathy were safe, I curled up under the duvet whispering the lyrics to 'Wuthering Heights' into a snoring Neil's ear, without him batting an eyelid. If only he knew the lucky escape he'd had tonight, he may well have rolled over and thanked me.

Chapter Nine: Women who munch

Somehow me and eccentric older ladies always got on. It's never been unusual for me to have senior friends forty years older than me who I simply adore. Usually, we'd find common ground in our animal rescue activities, or if not, some other form of connection would cement our togetherness. My tales of older female friends are never ending, especially ones who need rescuing with their furry friends, but others have danced into my heart with the true dedication to helping animals even into their nineties.

Sylvia Thoy was a great friend and fellow animal rescuer. Sylvia had been rescuing animals for decades. At her home lived a motley crew of second-hand dogs, ponies, goats, sheep, ducks, chickens, ferrets, rabbits, guinea pigs and a twenty-year-old swan named Lucy. Sylvia lived happily with her brood in a bungalow called Byways tucked away down a leafy unmade track near Sevenoaks, Kent. For many years she displayed a board at the top of her drive proudly advertising her animal rescue centre aptly named Tender Loving Care (TLC).

Life was good for all animals arriving at TLC because Sylvia had devoted her life mainly to stray dogs. Her Aga gently simmered her magic 'dog stew' that turned around the skinniest of strays within a week. The dogs had the free range of a well fenced large garden with the added bonus of what Sylvia called 'the gallop' The gallop was a narrow grass strip the full length of the property that gently sloped uphill from the nerve centre. Sylvia's pack of dogs covered all shapes and sizes and every known breed. Seniors and juniors could run freely together to their hearts content. It's not surprising, then, that Sylvia and I met over a great dog called Jasper.

Jasper was a young and lively border collie cross. With an outstanding black-and-white shiny coat, he was taller than most collies I had known, with long, thin, fluffy legs. Jasper wanted to be top dog and had started to boss his human family about. His low growls and snares were just the start of him throwing his weight around and if that didn't get his own way a nice bite with his pure white teeth to your leg or hand was delivered. Once Jasper had delivered his trump card, he was ever so sorry and would usually hide away from his terrified family. His family were growing more and more fearful with each show of his well-polished pegs. His last bite proved to be the family's last straw, and they decided he had to go that very night, no more chances. Without tears or remorse, they cold-heartedly called the vet to kill their furry family member.

I welcomed Jasper's arrival that evening after his reprieve from a kind-hearted veterinary nurse who refused to have him killed. I made him up somewhere cosy and quiet for the night. It didn't take him long to get his feet under the table and start to boss me around. He knew the bearing of his teeth was his winning card and I would always give in. One day not long after he arrived, he was happily chewing one of my work shoes and without thinking I leaned forward to take the shoe from him. Without hesitation, he bit my hand *hard*. His canine tooth went right through my thumbnail – it was agony.

At this time, I had a fair few dogs – just over forty in total. Most were not adoptable due to a snappy personality, but they'd very rarely bite their dad. My pack were happy to be left alone and live a comfortable dog life where I asked nothing from them. There were still rules – one being that *you do not eat my work shoes*. I had very little money, which was always spent no my animal family, so no spare cash for new shoes. 'Those shoes get me to work to put dog food on the table,' I'd have explained to them if I could.

Nursing my bleeding hand and my bruised pride, I washed it well under the running tap and between the throbbing pain and emotional heartache I realised I was now scared of Jasper too. I would have to find him somewhere else to live, somewhere more understanding of his naughtiness. Maybe he associated bad things with men, I was telling myself, trying to justify the decision to relocate Jasper. I had to accept that I'd lost my nerve with his unpredictable personality, and it was in Jasper's best interest that I found him somewhere to aid his healing. A rescue centre run by an older woman would be what we both needed, I contemplated.

The next day while Jasper stayed out of sight (chewing on a toy rather than my hand) I sat in the kitchen calling a list of established dog rescue numbers, only to be told by faceless professionals on the other end of the line that a biting dog couldn't be fixed and that the kindest thing to do would be to 'put him to sleep'. Feeling battered but not beaten, I carried on dialling number after number.

Just when the rejections were really starting to get to me, a breakthrough came. A well-spoken, kindly voice answered the phone just as I was about to give up. I was pleasantly surprised when, after explaining my situation, the voice at the other end of the line said 'Bring him over, have a cup of tea and let him meet the other dogs.'

Relieved, I jumped at the opportunity to pop over the following day and find out if this softly spoken angel had the magic wand to help Jasper. Once the woman had given me her address – only six miles up the road – and introduced herself as Sylvia Thoy, I immediately felt I had a friend.

The following day I arrived at the red brick bungalow hidden behind the usual row of village houses. When I turned off the engine, I could hear the distant song of barking dogs along with geese and calling goats. Jasper sat in the passenger seat, not at all bothered by the welcome call of Sylvia's menagerie. The front door had its key in the lock secured by a long piece of string that led back through the letterbox. Outside the front door was an assortment of critter enclosures from rabbit hutches to bird cages, fish tanks to pet carriers. There were also bales of hay, bags of sawdust, sacks of animal feeds and piles of carrots and lettuces – basically, anything an animal would need, and the real evidence that an animal rescuer lived here.

There was no need to knock the door; the animal occupants had alerted the landlady of TLC that someone had arrived. It wasn't long before the door opened slightly, and the almighty-of-animal-rescue stood in front of me. Already in her seventies, she glowed of goodness. Sylvia was very warm and welcoming and without thinking about it our friendship of mutual love for animals and a really good laugh had begun.

She summoned me to get Jasper out of the car and bring him in. Inside her home an assortment of hounds were awaiting the new kid. Larry Lurch the lurcher, Tara the bald German shepherd, Mr Glum a basset cross, Ellie and Lizzy two gently ageing German Shepherds and a wealth of other wagging tails lined the hall into the sitting room. Sylvia and I made our way to the arm chairs which looked out onto the dog garden, followed by the pony and goat paddocks and an impressive collection of hens, ducks and Sylvia's pride and joy Lucy the swan (then already in her twenties) My new friend had created an incredible hotel for stray and unwanted dogs on a journey to finding their forever homes.

We talked about our animal rescue histories and Sylvia told me she had been saving animals since the war when she was just a girl. During the blitz when the neighbours were evacuated or took to the air raid shelters, she would collect up the cats and dogs and even look after forgotten horses at her home in Crystal Palace, London. When she took the train from the railway station many strays accompanied her there and waited her return, then followed her back home. At this early stage I realised I was just the boy version of Mrs Thoy and we had so much more in common than we then realised.

Jasper was settled and after my umpteenth lemonade I decided it was time to leave him to start the next part of his journey at this rather luxurious kennel, a kind of Ritz

Hotel for strays. As I said my goodbyes, I knew Sylvia and I would be mates, cemented by this legend of the welfare scene offering me a helping hand. I touched base over the next few days and was given Jasper's latest update, like school reports. This was a real awakening for me, as I had to accept that I wasn't the right place for some really damaged animals, and I would need to learn how to draw a line under this rescue.

I visited TLC on the following Saturday and was not expecting just how quickly things had changed – but if I was really honest with myself, I wasn't surprised. Sylvia told me that Jasper had lunged for her twice but thankfully both times he had just missed. She had her serious face on, and I had a feeling a good talking-to was coming my way. Whilst she served me tea and then emptied a carrier-bag of the latest vegan goodies selected from her local Waitrose into my lap she was determined to convince me the best and safest thing for everyone was for Jasper to be euthanised. Obviously, that was never going to happen – I was that very person who stood between life and death and offered an alternative to those backed into a corner. It was that very day that Sylvia would stop killing dogs who failed their behavioural tests with her. From that day on TLC and The Retreat made a pact among the crisps, chocolate and mixed nuts; that I would take 'the sinners' (dogs not ready for adoption due to any kind of behavioural issues) from Sylvia and she would take any of mine who needed her magical build-up stew. A partnership formed from our tailored set of skills, in understanding of where every dog should start their recovery.

Over time, I learned so much from my twice monthly meetings with Sylvia, including many great tips for tracing and trapping lost and stray dogs. She worked so hard rescuing and rehoming many hundreds of dogs and other animals. During our long conversations sat in her comfortable lounge watching the many different birds on her buffet of hanging feeders, Sylvia would tell me the tales of a dear friend of hers who also was a great rescuer. Sadly, they had fallen out seven years ago over something very silly and hadn't spoken or seen each other since. Both women were in their early seventies and this felt horrid to me. I had no way of finding Sylvia's friend to try to mend the rift because she didn't want to share her details, thinking 'too much water under the bridge'. It was at this time our nicknames came about; mine for her was Girlfriend and she honoured our friendship by returning me the nickname Boyfriend.

By a strange and unbelievable coincidence, it wasn't long before I was contacted by a woman wanting to adopt some goats. The potential adopter told me of her great love for helping animals and the many she lived with. Pam sounded like an amazing home and we arranged to meet to discuss suitable animals to live alongside of her. Within the week I pulled up on Mrs Carrick's drive, never one to fail to find a good home for my many residents ready for their last stage of recovery. A friendly and cheeky woman in her sixties welcomed me in, surrounded by cats of every size and model. Pam loved all animals but had a special affinity with moggies, especially those unwanted ones. The three legged and one-eyed ones found love and care with Pam.

Pam showed me around her bungalow, home to every sort of creature, and then suggested she put the kettle on. She made me a strong black tea and we chatted away. She told me how she had rescued animals for years and given them everything, and eventually she mentioned a best friend she once had who she could have taken on some goats from had they still been friends. Something in me made the connection that this best friend Pam spoke

68

of could be my 'Girlfriend'. I waited for a pause to ask a very subtle question. The hurt in Pam's eyes as she spoke about her friend mirrored what I saw in Sylvia's when she had told me her story.

'How long haven't you spoken for?' I asked Pam.

'Seven years,' she replied emotionally and without hesitation. This was all the confirmation I needed to know that by some strange fate I was now sitting with Pam of Cudham, as Sylvia called her. How could I be the glue to fix this broken friendship after all these years?

I now knew how both 'the girls' were feeling, and I knew I had to do something – this incredible opportunity just couldn't be missed. I decided to come clean to Pam and tell her how well I knew Sylvia, how I knew that every day I spent with her she'd without a doubt mention how much she missed her friend Pam. Pam welled up and broke down, and we both cried together.

'What can I do?' she said. 'I've missed her so much.'

I comforted Pam and told her how I'd met 'Her Royal Highness' (my other nickname for Sylvia) during the time of Pam's absence.

'It was meant to be,' I explained to a red-eyed Pam, 'and once I've gone home you will call her tonight, the same time you always did before you fell out.' Pam looked worried, but I went on, 'Sylvia's been waiting seven long years now – just do it.'

At eight o clock that evening I got a thrilled phone call from Sylvia thanking me for working my magic. Her excitement was almost childlike, thrilled that their long and special friendship was back up and running like there'd been no gap at all. From that day on we were a rescue threesome sometimes joined by our other rescue hero Pauline, also from Cudham. Between us all we sorted out any animal crisis at any time night or day.

Sometimes the crisis could also be human animal. One

69

of my favourite Sylvia stories was when at the end of each day just before bedtime Sylvia would chat on the landline with her sister Evelyn covering all the events of the day. Sylvia's sister had been a driving instructor right into her nineties so between the two of them there would be many things to make them chuckle. This particular evening at just before midnight the sisters touched based as usual, but tonight there was a need for some outside help. Sylvia explained to Eve that for some reason her legs were so swollen that she couldn't pull her Wellingtons off. It didn't seem to matter what either of the girls did or suggested – the boots would not move. Growing more and more concerned, Eve suggested calling 999 for an ambulance to tend to her sister's mysteriously swollen legs.

Sylvia wanted no fuss. 'They'll be fine in the morning – I'll just have to sleep with the boots on,' she argued. Taking no more nonsense, Eve said goodbye, hung up and promptly dialled 999. She explained to the ambulance service her concerns about her elderly sister's medical mystery and the need for a rapid response. The control centre immediately dispatched an ambulance, and within twenty minutes the blue lights lit up the dark driveway.

Two very kind animal-loving paramedics climbed out and let themselves into the bungalow. Here, they found a bemused Sylvia now unable to get up out of the armchair, surrounded by her beloved canine family. After running some tests, both paramedics had to admit they weren't sure what had caused the problem. Baffled, the only respite they could offer was to cut off the boots and examine the swollen flesh below. With their best equipment, they worked out a way to cut down the tight rubber gripping the skin like a thick outer manmade protective layer. The boot slowly came apart, and the red blotchy epidermis spilled out. There was still no clue as to what the problem was, but, free from the pain, Sylvia thanked her two saviours for their time and patience. By now, it was the early hours and Mrs Thoy just needed her bed. She waved off the ambulance crew and climbed into bed, falling a sleep without another thought of the night's antics.

The next morning would bring unexpected answers to last night's mystery but not in the form of any major medical discovery. Sylvia's day started in its usual way with dogs being let out and given their breakfasts. Her old wellies laid useless by the armchair, sliced down their entire lengths, unfixable and needing to be thrown out. While Sylvia boiled the kettle on the Aga, she heard the front door go with her first visitor of the day, her great friend and helper Sharon.

Sharon was a great animal lover and used her time not only for her friendship with Sylvia but actively came to help care for those animals who lived at TLC. One of Sharon's regular jobs was to run the dogs up the gallop come rain or shine. Sharon was met by the welcome crew, all tails wagging, and a few warm barks of excitement. This greeting was like no other and Sharon clearly knew her job. A quick change of boots and out she usually went. She cast a quick glance to the side of the front door where her boots lived in her absence. Oddly enough only Sylvia's size nines stood waiting for her big feet, and Sharon's tiny size fives were missing.

Sylvia carried out the hot beverages and handed Sharon hers. Before Sharon could ask if the boss had seen her missing wellies, Sylvia started to tell her the ordeal of last night with the paramedics and how she didn't understand how she just couldn't get her boots off. Sharon began to smile and asked to see the dissected wellie boots. Sylvia handed them over from the bin and

Sharon turned them over to read the soles. There on the base of the boot was the answer to Sylvia's mysterious swelling: it said *size five*. Sharon's missing boots had been found and Sylvia's undiagnosed illness solved, all in one. Nobody was going to let her live it down, and it turned into one of our favourite of Mrs Thoy's stories. The only question that remained unanswered was how she ever got a tiny size five boot onto a gigantic size nine foot.

Sadly, my great friend passed away in 2018 following a short illness, but a funny story from her funeral ensured there were still time for a smile in true Sylvia style. During her funeral service where she lay-in-state up the front in a beautifully decorated coffin covered with images of German Shepherd dogs, a TV screen up high showed the most colourful photos of Sylvia's life including many of her rescues like Red Rum the Shetland pony and Lucy the swan, all of whom she had dedicated her later life to. Between the readings and a picture tribute, a very old lady played some familiar music on an organ. She looked over at me and noticed how upset I was during the service, even though I was tucked away at the back with Neil. Once the final lines of the service had been read, the mourners stood up and started to file out. There wasn't a single dry eye in the house. Sylvia was irreplaceable, and she was far too big a friend for us to recover from this loss.

I hung back and let the chapel empty. Remembering the fun Sylvia and I had had just made it harder. The white-knuckle rides in her van while looking for lost dogs, my heart almost stopping as the eighty-five-year-old took corners at speeds matching her age, like Stirling Moss. I walked slowly to her coffin with my heart broken and crying uncontrollably. I just needed a minute to make sense of it, death that is. Yes, I understand that it's the price we pay for love, but it's a heavy one. Unable to conceal my sadness, my tears dropped onto the polished floor, my eyes stinging from the soreness of crying my eyes out. I leaned forward and kissed the face of a proud German shepherd dog, just like those Sylvia had when we first met. My body shook and I held the coffin to steady me. My head swirling with memories, I thought about how much I was going to miss my old mate.

At this point I noticed something to my right. I rubbed my face and stared at the object through my watery eyes, and realised it was the tiny organ player crying with me.

'I noticed you crying uncontrollably earlier, and I can see you're still hurting. Was she someone close to you?' asked the woman.

'She was my "girlfriend",' I proudly replied. I could see in the musician's face that this seemed odd – me forty-nine years old, my girlfriend ninety-one. Explaining our friendship seemed insurmountable at this point. 'It's just our nicknames.' The organ player gave me a strange smile and I could see she was trying to work it all out. In a sweet gesture she kindly took my arm and escorted me out to meet the others.

RIP Sylvia Thoy, 5th February 1927–21st January 2018.

Chapter Ten: Gilbert and the magician

Dating was a preoccupation of my full-time rescue world. Saving animals and my gang came first, with no close second. Everyone seemed to find their other half in an orthodox manner like from school, college or work, but my whole life was more of a jigsaw puzzle with all things needing to fit in around other bits. There were many missed opportunities which I easily shrugged off due to one too many stray dogs or dying foals but occasionally voila, I'd get lucky (well, lucky for me).

Long before the days of internet searching for a bride or groom, we had to rely on the good old fashioned 'catching of an eye', and this could happen literally anywhere. On dog walks, catching a train, or even in the alcohol aisle of a supermarket.

Safeway was my local supermarket, and back in the day there were virtually no mainstream vegan items, apart from those in the fruit and veg department. My usual shopping trip went like this: I'd turn up ten minutes before closing to ensure I bagged a bargain for my rescue family. It would take me no more than about six minutes to cruise the deserted store in search of the very best 'reduced to clear' products at the end of every row. My weekly supplies consisted of mountains of special-offer tinned cat and dog food, fresh fruit and vegetables at the end of their display date, dried pasta, expired bread, value crackers and the essential dented tin of 'saver's' baked beans, and the week's lifesaving cheap Chianti. The car park was almost always empty so I would leave my Fiat Panda unlocked (no one in their right mind would steal her), parked next to the entrance and within easy reach to grab a trolley and start the challenge.

In a scene that would have beaten any Supermarket Sweep leaving the gorgeous Dale Winton with G-force sores on his bronzed face, I set off like Usain Bolt. Still singing to Culture Club's 'Do You Really Want to Hurt Me?' which had been playing on the car radio, I layered the bottom of the trolley with the trays of tinned food, then covered it with a natural filling of colourful fruit and veg – iceberg lettuce was a good buy today at only a penny each. Next came the dried goods with a stock up on cream-crackers, bourbon creams, crisps and then onto the important bit: the wine. I headed for the 'Reds'.

Occasionally there would be a shelf packer in the store, who would recognise me and call out an obliging 'How's the animals?', to which I'd reply, 'Another four cats this week!' but wouldn't stop to hear the response. Tonight was very different, and I had to slow down because standing in front of the Italian Reds was a very well-dressed man. I was a naïve and friendly twenty-three-year-old who at any other time would normally stop and chat to anyone. It was a running joke that the reason we didn't have donkeys at The Retreat was because I'd talk their hind legs right off – though how wrong were those who said such things when Pat, Peter, Joey and Eeyore my donkeys remained mobile and still had their hind legs.

Now, back to the wine isle. The dapper chap stood between me and my much-needed Chianti. He was holding a very fine bottle of vino from a higher shelf as if he'd been handed his first born and was admiring the miracle of life. I leaned in to reach for two bottles, not wanting to disturb his precious moment. He stepped back, apologising profusely and I responded that it wasn't a problem, then charmed him with my extensive wine knowledge that he could get three bottles of Chianti for the price tag of his bottle. I'd noticed how handsome this connoisseur of the grape was but remembering my time frame I gave a toothy grin and tried to take off. He held the front of the trolley and stared in at my staples.

'Do you have a lot of rabbits?' he asked, picking up one of my penny icebergs. 'And, goodness, how many cats and dogs do you have?' Monsieur Vin Rouge was very well turned out including a very good dark suit, crisp dark blue shirt and well-polished laced-up black shoes. Golden cufflinks of musical notes glistened in the strip lightning. His dark black hair and beard were finely manicured, adding the final touches to his immaculate appearance. I on the other hand always looked like I'd been 'pulled through the hedge backwards'. Second-hand clothes either too big or too small, trousers looking like they had divorced my ankles and married my knees or gigantic shirts that would not have been out of place coming from rent-a-tent. Slip-on shoes with no socks and some recycled jewellery made of copper wire twisted to make rings and bangles. Bohemian I was and never ever even slightly smart, so this was a case of chalk and cheese coming together over good old-fashioned common ground, wine. This I thought would never be a case of mutual attraction more a case of politeness when caught off guard. Anyway, who was to know at first that he was also a 'friend of Dorothy'? I've never had a good 'Gaydar' (gay radar).

I steered my trolley of treasurers around Mr Suited and Booted's wire basket of Safeway's finest wines and bid him goodnight. I scooted off and found the only cashier sitting bored and ready to go home, waiting rather restlessly for the last few shoppers to exit the store. My army of tin cans and limp lettuces made their way along the conveyor belt. Julie the cash-out girl smiled at me and added if I'd acquired any more animals since I was last in. Of course, I happily answered back 'Yes, many!' and we both laughed. I boxed my shopping up and piled it back into my trolley and took off to the car park at a great speed.

I opened the boot of the car and pushed back a layer of dog leads, muddy boots and horse brushes to accommodate my supplies. While I messed around organising the car, the store's automatic doors opened and out came Blackheath's answer to George Clooney. *Ooh la la,* I sang in my head, smiling his way. To my utter surprise, he stopped and delved into his shopping bag. Pulling out one of his bottles of wine, he handed it to me.

'For you,' he said. 'Try it, it is really rather good.' But before I reached forward to take it, he went on, 'I'm completely intrigued – why so many lettuces?'

He's never going to believe that the many different creatures living with me love them, I thought to myself. From the rats and squirrels to the hens, and even Prince, the pure white peacock who I had recently acquired. *How do I explain where they all live?* I decided to be a tad flippant, and just mentioned that I had some 'pets'. I hesitantly accepted the fine wine, convinced by its gold label that it must be worth the price, and offered him a penny iceberg in exchange.

'No,' he said, waving his hand. 'I wouldn't deprive the animals.'

'Come on, it's only one iceberg – and not the one that sunk the Titanic,'

'Now *that's* an icebreaker,' he joked back. I banged the boot shut on tonight's shopping, marking the end of our exchange.

The man casually took out his swanky wallet and produced his business card. *How impressive,* I thought, still with a smile on my face. I then caught sight of his name, standing out in gold print on the black card: Gilbert.

'Call me and let me know if you liked the wine,' Gilbert said, not at all hesitant in coming forward. I jumped into the driver's seat and took off, thinking what a cheeky chappie Mr Cool was.

My weeks were busy with the life-saving calls of animals who needed my help, then work and the general things life finds to surprise you with. Tonight was different. I found myself among the usual crew of dog walkers in Greenwich park, having a relaxed walk and a good catch-up with everyone. The faces of the other dog walkers were familiar to me, and although I didn't know them individually, I named them in my head after either their dog's breed or name: Mr Cocker, Mrs Lab, Mr and Mrs Poodle, Mrs Cassie the Collie and Mr Paddy Boxer. We talked everything dog, from vet's fees to newly found dog walks, our canine companions' favourite food and even the condition of our dog stools.

When our walk came to an end and we all parted company I reached into my coat pockets for the mass of dog leads I had stuffed deep down inside. As I pulled the tangled pile of leashes free, the black and gold business card from my Safeway encounter flicked out, landing among the motley crew of canine companions. Staring up at me was the glistening gold inscription: *Gilbert*. I took this as a sign, and decided that once everyone at home was settled tonight, I would call Gilbert to talk red wines.

To settle the hounds of Blackheath down for the evening was no easy job: growls, snares, barks and stand offs over the best beds took some time to calm down. Not always did the biggest meanest looking mutt win either; sometimes the little fierce and firm Lovejoy the miniature black and tan dachshund would be crowned top bed winner of the evening. All this going on with Libby the tiniest Shetland pony trying to find her sleeping zone amongst her unlikely herd who lived in the flat too.

Libby was just a tiny foal when I found her on a rubbish pile in Woolwich, South East London. Her dirty and tangled black and white hairy coat disguising the saddest thin frame. Covered with lice and fighting the killer Equine Influenza, she was too weak to stand. I simply picked up the twenty-kilo foal and carried her to the car. Back at the flat I cleaned her sore eyes and nose with warm water and cotton wool and offered her a warm bottle of milk. I could sense that Libby was already feeling better from having the comfort of a warm bed, and for the life-sucking parasites having been treated with a gentle warm shower in my bath. She now sported a fine mane and forelock, and it hadn't taken her long to readily take her bottles and grow in strength. She raced around the flat with the dogs, running up and down the stairs until exhausted. She now knew that her rescue vehicle was also the one to take her out somewhere nice with the dogs, too. As far as Libby was concerned, she may as well have been one of the dogs.

Once everyone was settled and flat out snoring, I took the business card out and without a second thought I dialled the number. There were no mobiles back then, and my house phone was a big plastic pay-phone box; it required you to drop coins into the slot to make calls. All silver coins were accepted, and I kept a pile of fifty pence pieces for callers to use. I could unlock the box and use the funds inside if I ever ran out – meaning the contents never covered the phone bill when it arrived.

The phone was answered on the seven ring, by a deep unsuspecting voice.

'Hello?'

'It's Billy – with the lettuces and the very good bottle of red wine,' I said. Our conversation got off to a good start, with many fast and funny one-liners. Gilbert was a natural with the charm offenses and it wasn't long before he took the opportunity to ask me out on a date. I could hear him drinking his velvety wine while I sat under a pile of purring cats, balancing my cup of tea and surrounded by sleeping dogs. Each time the tone sounded for me to put in more money, I juggled the coins, manoeuvred the cats and piled in the fifty pence coins. Gilbert heard the clank of the coins as they dropped, the noise echoing from the chamber, and asked if somebody was playing backgammon in the background.

Backgammon? Wasn't that for posh people? 'Yes,' I replied. Our chat continued until I made an excuse about somebody at the door, asking if Gilbert could call me back in fifteen minutes as the last of the coins ran out. Gilbert called me back dead on time, and the conversation continued without the interruption of 'backgammon' overshadowing us. It didn't take much longer for Gilbert to start chatting details of the date, expressing his love for fine art and good wine. I managed to persuade him to think of something a bit more suitable for us both – maybe a play, or a show. We said our goodnights after several hours of small talk and agreed to speak again the following night.

Gilbert was a hoot, and a man of many talents, but for me the winning trait was that he was also an animal lover. This made me interested in taking things a little further. Over the next few weeks we met for several drinks and a few dinner dates. His sense of humour was as captivating as his dress sense. Our mutual love of animals seemed to gel us together in spite of all our other differences. The unifying magic of animals never fails to cross any barrier, whether that be religion, age or politics.

Gilbert arranged a night out for us in central London. We would meet after work and go and see a famous magician work some real magic on a theatre of sceptics. It wasn't really my thing, but I enjoyed Gilbert's company and hearing all about his wildlife experiences across the globe. He was an old romantic and knew just how to lay on a very impressive date.

I took the train to Charing Cross dressed in the smartest of choices from my wardrobe of second-hand best buys. My odd socks were hidden under very long trousers (a first), and I wore a cat-hair covered shirt below a buttoned jacket. My mantra that night was *I must remember not to take off my jacket or undo the buttons to reveal my secret*...I was really a very hairy werewolf.

The train was full of interesting types heading uptown for a Friday night of drinks with friends, watching a play, going to a gig or an overnight stay in one of the greatest capitals of the world. London really does have something for everyone and should leave no one disappointed. I jumped off the train with a spring in my step, knowing I too would not be disappointed by tonight's entertainment. I followed the highly charged crowd through the turnstiles and out towards the taxi ranks. While everyone hurried off to their chosen form of enjoyment for the night, I noticed a trio of young pigeons huddled together in the spot where the homeless people of London would later be making up their beds for the night. The trio looked grubby and unwell, and any pigeon on the ground at night is sure to set alarm bells ringing for any rescuer.

My dilemma was not whether or not I'd rescue the babies, but what I would do with them. The little black skinny birds were surprisingly happy to be scooped up and held safely in warm hands. For a few seconds I stood forlornly, thinking I'd need a box or a bag so that I could meet Gilbert as planned. All other options failed, so I decided to tuck the birds in my jacket under my arm, where they would feel more secure and receive my body heat. I opened two buttons and placed the birds into the makeshift nest of an armpit, cat hair and all.

I waved a taxi and climbed inside, giving the driver my destination from an awkward sitting position, trying not to wake the babies. As the taxi weaved through the busy London streets, I wondered what I could do with the babies until my date was over. My brainstorm produced no results, so I had no choice but to secretly carry my new friends along with me. The taxi pulled in just in front of a well-turned-out Gilbert who stood waiting for me to arrive. I paid my fare and emerged onto the pavement like Cinderella arriving at the ball – both Cinderella and I concealing the truth of the evening.

Gilbert had everything lined up: drinks in a swanky cocktail bar, then we'd go on to see the best magician in town.

'Are you okay?' he asked. 'You seem a little tense – which isn't like you.'

'I'm fine, just a little stressed about wanting to get here on time,' I said. Not wanting to disappoint Gilbert after all his effort and kindness, I said nothing of my stowaways. I felt like everyone in the bar could see how awkwardly I was behaving. I didn't dare move my left arm in case I disturbed the sleeping trio, but I lifted my glass with my right hand and made the most of the happy atmosphere. After a few drinks we left the bar and chatted as we walked to the theatre. Inside, we grabbed another drink and headed for our seats.

Our seats were mid-auditorium with a very fine view. A middle-aged married couple to my right made small talk about how great the magician was, having read the latest reviews. The wife asked me if my dad had brought me here for a treat.

'He's kind of my boyfriend,' I replied. 'We're on a date.' A mortified look crossed her face and she turned back to her husband, downing her gin and tonic in one. Gilbert removed his jacket and laid it over the back of his chair, in the tidy manner in which he did everything. While he was standing he offered to help me out of my jacket, too, but I told him I was still cold and would prefer to stay wrapped up for now.

'It's very warm in here,' Gilbert reassured me. Both he

and the woman next to me (who was now eavesdropping) stared at me, baffled as I looked so out of place. A puzzled Gilbert settled down, wanting reassurance that I really was okay. Inside my jacket, the occasional stirring informed me that everyone was still alive and kicking. This brought a smile to my face, which Gilbert would catch in the stage lights.

Nothing too epic was happening when the magician's sidekick asked for some audience participation: 'We need three participants to stand up and help us with a hypnotism exercise.' Within seconds, two volunteers had been chosen, and the assistant searched the crowd for a third. Mortified, I realised the main man on stage was pointing at me, thinking my coolness (though I was actually overheating under my jacket) and lack of participation was an indication of my scepticism over his 'skills'.

'No, no, no,' I protested, pointing to Gilbert for him to participate instead. Everyone was now pointing, staring, clapping or mouthing encouragement at me, so with the help of both of my seated neighbours I was begrudgingly encouraged to stand up like the other two chosen ones. The room fell silent under the command of the modern-day wizard, and the nearest chosen one was brought to the stage and asked his name under a single spotlight.

'Frank,' the man replied. The magician then hypnotised Frank into thinking he was an elephant. Frank played along, spurting water from his 'trunk' which was created by pushing his arm against his face, waving it around to strange noises. The tasks continued with roars of laughter from the crowd. The second victim, Mary, took centre stage, and another show of similarly silly tricks followed. By the time my turn came around, my babies had warmed up and were a little active inside my outer garments.

The spotlight fell onto me, and once again the wizard achieved absolute silence. He asked my name before demanding I fell into a standing sleep and responded to his instructions.

'*You are a huge redwood tree swaying in the wind.*' This was not my cup of tea, and I was under no illusion that I was a great tree. I could see Gilbert staring up at me, and Mrs G&T in the chair next to mine. The wizard tried a little more persuasive language. Not wanting to be a killjoy, I lifted my arms above my head and pretended to sway in the strong winds. Through the darkness I could see the faces of the many believers, bursting with joy that I was finally under the main man's spell. Without any warning, the first of the pigeons burst out from under my jacket to see what all the fuss was about. You could have heard a pin drop – and then the second musketeer appeared. The gasping audience, witness to real magic, could not believe their luck. Within seconds, the final musketeer stepped onto his stage (my shoulder). At this point, Gilbert must have thought he was dreaming, and Mrs G&T was on the point of passing out. The magician must have thought he was the chosen one – *at last, my magic is working!* – the blank expression on his face said it all. There I stood for all to see, a swaying tree in the wild winds, decorated by authentic birds who were just the icing on the cake. I grabbed my new friends and popped them back inside my jacket, then hurried back to Gilbert.

'We'd better leave,' I said to Gilbert. The curtain came down and the lights came on, and an ecstatic crowd stamped their feet with joy. Mrs G&T looked disappointedly at me.

I had some explaining to do to dear pale Gilbert. On our journey home after the shock had worn off and a smile crept back to his recovering face, he told me he wasn't really that surprised. He had questioned whether this could really be magic, thinking how disappointed I'd be if they were using real pigeons. Although our relationship didn't go any further; maybe I was full of one too many surprises: our love for all animals including pigeons just strengthened our bond. Gilbert the Great is still a great supporter of my quest to rescue everyone. He's now just across the border from me in East Sussex with his own menagerie of creatures great and small, adopted from The Retreat.

Chapter Eleven:
The land of the lost promise

When I look back to the iconic films of my youth, I'm always transported back to the sadness of how humans let animals and vulnerable people down. I've never re-watched *King Kong*. I imagined what it could be like if explorers were to find 'Nessie' the Loch Ness Monster, or Bigfoot the Yeti. Just like the fictional Kong, they too would be exploited and ultimately killed. One of the saddest stories is that of the Elephant Man, the true story of the amazing John Merrick. And don't get me started on *Black Beauty* or *Watership Down*. These great time pieces, with their hidden messages of failed humanity, should have prepared me for my path into the villainous world of animal rescue.

Incredibly, animal rescue foundations are built on the generosity of people who will never need their services. But imagine this: the people actually in need of your service will often 'donate' their animals to you, time and time again, and never part with a penny. This means that almost every animal taken in to The Retreat will come without a single penny of support. Horses, cows, sheep and pigs are brought to the rescue by their guardians who never give a second thought to how the enormous monthly running costs are funded. Most arrive without a single bag of food. Even better, we're sometimes told that their medication's just run out, while these 'owners' cry tsunamis of crocodile tears.

I've been promised planet earth by people in need of my help. They usually look at our latest fundraiser and say 'I see you're trying to purchase more land – I can help you with that,' or 'If you look after my cats for six months I promise I'll pay you hundreds monthly for their care.' These promises are never fulfilled. People will even fill out standing order forms in support of our work, using phoney bank details. These people are real scammers, and they know how to fool those who have only the best intentions. To be a bad person must take such effort. Why not just tell the truth, and say 'I'm sorry, but I can't support my animal anymore'? I've had people say ridiculous things, claiming their millionaire uncle will buy us a new tractor or something equally farfetched. For so many decades, I've heard the same old statement: 'You're in my will, so please help me with my animal now,' even when there are no funds and no will.

We all know of those who will lose a relative and will take the dog or cat who provided the deceased companionship for their last few years will immediately be taken along to a local shelter, while they receive the many material assets belonging to their loved ones. Day in, day out, many older people rely on a furry companion to keep them active and keep loneliness at bay. Their dear friend of many years will have been fed the best foods, shared their bed and smiled at them every morning as they woke up, only to be sent away without another thought.

The land of lost promise is not just in those empty promises to the animals you know, but also those you don't – and these are the ones who need us most. People who give up being vegetarian or vegan turn their backs on billions of animals who are living a life of hell, locked away in the dark, treated in a way these people once knew to be wrong – so when did it become 'right'? Their feeble excuses include 'I was on holiday and there was nothing to eat.' 'So there are countries where there are no vegans?' I reply. Another is 'My boyfriend didn't want to cook two meals,' buy why not both try eating vegan?

Other 'animal donors' become angry when they call up months later asking about their 'pet', only to learn they have been adopted by a far more suitable home. '*How dare you get rid of my animal? I wanted them to stay at your place forever,*' or '*You told me you'd never give my pet away*' are common responses. The lack of commitment to animals is all part of the job. You keep smiling, thinking always of the animals. Everyday there's another 'animal lover' parting with five cats with new puppy under their arm.

We deal with this day in, day out, and there is only one way to do so: by taking the professional approach, even if a little sarcasm does occasionally creep in. One instance of this is a woman who turned up claiming to have found several pigs in a lane. It turned out she lived three doors down, and her husband turned up with *more* pigs a few weeks later.

'Amazing the animals know where to find you,' I said to him. But you do it for the pigs; you get them safe and settled, and let the people abandoning their animals think they've got one over on you. Nothing matters but the animals and their future. I could fill a book with stories of the lost promise, but sometimes they're better off forgotten. Animals are let down so often outside the protection of genuine animal rescue. Remember Geronimo the alpaca, who made national news when he tested positive for TB? The British government makes no exception for any creature that falls outside of their guidelines. The campaign to save him by the great British public was lost before it started and poor Geronimo was violently seized then driven away to be killed in a slaughterhouse. Later his autopsy results proved – just like with millions of other creatures – that his TB status was incorrect and in fact Geronimo was negative. There were no apologies and no scrutiny of those who ripped him away from the people who cared about him. This happens to cattle almost daily, and there is no sad outcry for them.

TB testing is just another case of failed or phony silence, at the cost of wonderfully kind animals. At the same time as Geronimo's unjust killing, we also saw West Ham footballer Kurt Zouma attack his two cats. He later received a fine and his cats were removed, but he wasn't fired from the club – a great message to be sending to young people who follow the club, to show that they are okay with such cruelty towards animals.

These acts of animal abuse were also followed by the 'respected' international show-jumper Mark Todd being dropped by major horse charities after he was filmed being cruel to a horse in public. Then pony club secretary and schoolteacher Sarah Moulds was charged for two offences after being filmed beating and kicking a pony at a local pony club event, and was rightly fired. Yet good people like Pen Farthing (an ex Royal Marine turned animal rescuer) whose charity Nowzad helps animals escape the horrors of life on the street in Afghanistan was completely vilified for evacuating the residents of his centre by plane when the British government gave back rule to the Taliban. The whole of his journey for animals hijacked by people who needed their daily dose of hate and spreading misinformation, including at the time The Secretary of State Ben Wallace. Mr Wallace did his best to discredit Pen by stating the plane used to rescue animals should have been used to evacuate people. He believed that, in war, there is no room for animals or sentiment. At every level, Mr Wallace and other animal haters did their best to throw mud, but international animal-loving warriors took to social media and mounted a bigger 'Pen's a hero and Wallace a zero' campaign. There were even crowdfunds launched to pay for the plane.

The minister knew no humans could fly in the hold of that plane, only the animals. Mr Wallace could have worked with Pen to ensure the seats of that plane had people sitting in them, but instead he carried out his hate campaign against Pen and the good Afghan people of Nowzad. People like Mr Wallace do nothing for people either; haters only have hate, nothing more, nothing less. Why can't animals be equal to humans in their own intricate way, I ask?

It's also not unusual to find cruelty, misery, neglect and death within the rescue movements of many so-called animal rescue projects. Animal sanctuaries have had their founders exposed, and many prosecuted. Sarah Ross from The Animal Sanctuary UK was taken to court and received a five-year ban on keeping animals – later reduced at appeal to one year – for dreadful neglect. Initially I'd been a defender of Mrs Ross, and it took me some time to realise the wool was being pulled over my eyes. The Alternative Animal Sanctuary run by Tamara Lloyd was another case of a carer turned abuser, being struck off by a regulator and found guilty of sixteen animal welfare offences, with dogs, cats, horses and pigs being kept in appalling conditions.

Other rescue projects run single-handedly by people who never let anyone in through the gates have been found to contain fields of sick and malnourished forgotten pigs, some crushed to death by fallen haystacks. Instructions to throw boiling water over fighting dogs were common policy for new volunteers. This sanctuary 'owner' escaped prosecution and even a ban on keeping animals, but animal rights activists were able to remove the neediest animals and offer an action plan.

There are also what we call 'policy killings', a blanket rule to kill animals arriving at so-called rescue centres. The RSPCA condones the killing of non-indigenous wildlife such as ruddy ducks, ring-necked parakeets, terrapins and grey squirrels. They have also made headlines for the killing of twelve German shepherd dogs by captive bolt (gun), and even for killing a young deer who had become too tame to be released. Other national 'animal homes' carry out blanket killings of certain dog breeds, and cats with the odd blood disorder like FIV, even though they can live healthily to an old age with it.

The notion that the UK is a nation of animal lovers is complete folly. We are more 'pet obsessed' than animal lovers. Most 'pet obsessed' people will do anything for their beloved companion, spending thousands at the vet's on the latest treatments (as they should), such as chemotherapy, prosthetic limbs, hydrotherapy and organ transplants. This is all well and good, but most of these people will then go home and eat the flesh or body parts of another murdered animal. The animal on their plate was no different to their 'pet'; capable of being loved, and not fearful of returning it. Sadly, the dinner-plate corpse was a beautiful young animal with his whole life in front of him. After the stress of the journey to the slaughterhouse, the hell which greets them inside will include gassing, throat-cutting, electric shock and boiling

90

– not exactly the actions of animal lovers.

Those of us who really believe in justice for animals and love our companion animals just like our human family members would give absolutely anything for a little bit of extra time with them before they go to Rainbow Bridge (heaven, where all animals are equal and live their best lives). I've never seen animals as disposable objects whose individual lives don't matter, because I truly know animals and their lives really do matter to them, just like yours do to you. We must be eternally grateful to all those who stand by rescue centres and the animals who need them.

Chapter Twelve: Sweet dog street dog

Not everywhere is the faithful dog man's best friend. There are approximately six hundred million dogs on the earth right now – more than enough for everyone who wants a dog without breeding anymore. Crossbreds come with less illness, and fewer hereditary problems, and they cost a whole lot less to take into your home, too. Adoption fees go back into funding more animal rescues, whilst breeders live off their ill-gotten gains.

The most fashionable dog currently seems to be the French bulldog. Certain colours and breeds of French bulldog can cost anywhere from £4,000 to £10,000, and sadly most of these dogs will require a costly operation to free up their airways. After paying such a price for a dog, most owners will not cover the cost of surgery, so these sad, badly bred companions often make their way into rescue while struggling to breathe.

I now share my home with street dogs from Mauritius,

Romania, Bosnia, Macedonia, Bahrain, Greece, Turkey, Lithuania, Ireland and the UK. As a write this, Bear, a large black-and-white herding-type dog with no eyes sleeps carefree by my feet. At only three months old, he was found in the remote Bulgarian countryside, having clearly been dumped. He was already blinded by a terribly painful eye infection and would have starved to death. Thankfully, he was rescued and sent to the UK, where both eyes were removed to give him a pain-free life. Nothing stops this boy from having an incredibly active life where he runs free and swims in the sea and any lake he can sniff out. He plays with his best friend Douglas from Romania for hours and sleeps in a pile of dog mates too.

Adopting a street dog – or another animal – is one of the best things you can ever do. Not only will you be saving a life, but given time, your street dog will become the sweetest dog ever. Many have witnessed unimaginable horrors, including deliberate cruelty from dogcatchers, or survived government and private dog-holding facilities. Dogs rescued from such places have escaped disease, injury, starvation and death, whether that be by other dogs, electrocution gassing, brutality or – if you're lucky – one lethal injection.

When you adopt your sweet dog from the streets of some far away land remember most will never have travelled before. For dogs coming over from Macedonia will have travelled up to four days overland and dogs from as far as Mauritius the journey will be twenty-four hours including airport red tape and flight. These dogs need to decompress when they arrive with you, with at least three weeks at home just eating and sleeping – no immediate walks or visits to family, pet stores or groomers. They need to know their home, know they're safe and build trust with their new parent. This way, their life will start relaxed and trusting, with a 'slowly does it' approach. I've heard of people deciding they no longer want their new international companion, because after an hour they're still hiding behind a sofa, or because they snap when their new owner's husband tries to fit a harness on them.

I remember finding a group of twenty-four abandoned dogs on wasteland in Portugal many years ago. In pursuit of a poor and matted dog, I left the car on foot and followed him to the local dumping ground of 'ex-pet' territory. I couldn't believe my eyes: it was a starving colony of wagging tails, many dogs still wearing their sparkling collars from when they were a fashion accessory with an address. In desperation, I ran back to the car to get food and help.

On arriving at the car, I saw someone was sitting at the driver's seat. At first, I thought someone was stealing the car – silly me, leaving the driver's door open. Now, a massive Great Dane-type dog sat slobbering over the steering wheel. I moved the large friendly black-and-tan dog into the back of the car and set off to the vets and supermarket. I now had a huge, loving companion, who was very glad to have been rescued, and not a joyrider as I'd initially thought.

To my astonishment, the vet actually knew the dog and said 'Great, you found Ozzie – his English owner died and Ozzie was given away by friends.' Because of Ozzie's size and looks, his new home wanted him for a guard dog. The vet went on to tell me Ozzie was so unhappy he had chewed through his long rope and escaped. Nobody had seen him until now.

The good news was that Ozzie had a passport and could travel back to the UK with me. Now, all I needed to do was feed the strays and come up with a plan to get them to safety. I cleared the shelves of the local supermarket and filled the back of my car with everything the dogs needed. Where would I start? Feeding and water was part one of the operation. Then I would decide on names, and who would go to the vet first to be neutered, blood tested, vaccinated and issued with a 'pet passport' to travel next.

The dogs were named based on who or what they looked like. A small black girl with stuck-up ears became Pixie, and the interested fluffy white girl with her head in a box became Pandora. The red-and-white boy who nipped the back of my leg became Nipper, and the smallest terrier cross Tiny. The medium boy with a flat face became Boxer, and the matted black dog of course became Scruffy – and so on. All the veterinary procedures went well, and a plan was formed to move the dogs to the safety of a shelter outside Portugal. My helpers were mainly German, and before long we had a brilliant contact in Hamburg. Sabrina was a great animal rescuer, and she agreed to take all the dogs if I could fund the travel. With my credit cards all maxed out on the vet care and food for the dogs, I needed to get home and appeal to the Bank of Mum and Dad for funds to help the dogs.

With the vets preparing the other dogs for travel, I returned to the UK with my new best friend Ozzie. Ozzie made the national news with his inspirational rescue story, and he and I were inseparable. On one occasion, I took him with me to drop off my nephew at school, and in the six minutes he spent alone in the car he chewed up all five head rests, *and* three seatbelts, to add to his resume of destruction. It wasn't long before he found his forever home with friends of The Retreat Annabelle and Adrian and lived his best life. After securing funds from the best parents in the world, all the abandoned dogs could now travel and await their forever homes with Sabina in Hamburg. The wasteland was finally developed into homes and a network of great rescue friends formed.

One final note in my testimonial to these sadly let down yet great companions. Let no one tell you that street dogs don't deserve our compassion and help. For those hampering the efforts of good people helping street dogs worldwide are not animal lovers but dangerous obstacles in our battle to ensure every dog gets the care they deserve wherever they may live in this world. Adopt today for a better tomorrow and make it a sweet dog street dog – you won't be disappointed.

Chapter Thirteen:
The Great Jewel Thief

It was December the twenty-third, a very busy Christmas time in Central London, with the streets packed with busy shoppers and international tourists admiring the traditional English Christmas. The shops were beautifully decorated, with smiling tellers welcoming you inside. This year's magical Christmas lights of Oxford Street and Regent Street had been turned on, and the display made children look up in wonder.

I was not a tourist or a shopper but was demonstrating outside a fur shop on Oxford Street called Nobel Furs of London. The plan was to educate any potential shopper about the horrors of the fur industry and discuss other more ethical products to buy. Usually the police were well tempered but today a combination of light rainfall, the heavily polluted London air and the mass arrests of opportunist criminals had put the officers at the demonstration in a particularly bad mood. Each wet protester was warned that if we stepped out of line, we would be arrested and held for maximum time in the local station.

One policeman was arguing with me about obstruction and disturbing the peace. When he could not correctly quote the law to me, he grabbed me and pushed me into another officer. 'You're nicked,' he said, to boos and hisses from my fellow protestors. The angry copper shrugged them off, refusing to back down. I was pushed into a patrol car and a few minutes later we turned the corner into West End Central Police Station, with no explanation as to the crime I had committed. The officer escorting me into the station informed me that he was arresting me under section whatever of the public order act, almost an afterthought to his action.

'How silly,' I replied, smiling.

I was processed by a polite desk sergeant, who I could see was truly embarrassed by the officers' actions. 'It's extremely busy,' he remarked, 'and we're already doubling up on cells just as long as the animal rights lot don't share.' My cell door opened, and it wasn't empty either. Inside, a smartly dressed guy in his thirties (a little older than me) sat rubbing his hands like they were hurting and sucking a sweet, a plastic cup of black coffee beside him.

'What have they thrown you in for?' he asked with interest, in an Italian accent. 'Is that even a crime?' he asked after I explained my arrest, looking totally baffled. He then smiled in what I thought might be solidarity. 'The coffee's terrible – it tastes like pond water. The English don't know how to make coffee.'

'I'm not sure you visit police stations for their coffee making skills,' I replied, and the man laughed. I asked the man why he was spending his time in here and not some upmarket bar with an experienced barista.

'Well, they say I've stolen something!'

'Have you?' I asked.

'No, of course not. I'm not like that.'

Next came our introduction. 'I'm Billy, by the way.'

'Giuseppe.'

I imagined Giuseppe to be a moneyed man, maybe even a millionaire. He was finely turned out in a tailored suit, with highly polished shoes and the air of an Italian fashion house owner. Of course, he wouldn't steal anything – why would he? He then asked me how he could see a doctor for his hands, as though I was a hardened criminal used to a day 'banged up'. He had broken skin around the wrists where he had been forcibly handcuffed.

I reassured Giuseppe that I would call someone to get a doctor. The only way to get any attention was to continually shout out until someone arrived. After a few minutes, I gave up with a sore throat and red hands from banging on the cell door. Giuseppe was grateful for my efforts and offered me his last remaining sweet from his lapel pocket.

'Yes please,' I replied. 'How did you manage to hide that from the officers?'

A smile crept across Giuseppe's face. 'I'm not stupid,' he replied.

The police were dealing with an influx of Christmas drunks, petty thieves, ladies of the night, fly pitchers (street sellers with no license), and of course, my fellow activists. Still no obliging officer came, so we continued with our small talk. After a few minutes, my over-active imagination and desperate curiosity got the better of me, and I needed to know the terrible allegations made against this seemingly innocent man (after all, we'd now been friends for three hours'.

I remarked to my cell mate that the alleged theft must have been serious for him to have been handcuffed and thrown into jail. He thought for a moment, allowing for an awkward silence while he contemplated his reply. He then faced me like I was his judge and jury.

'Okay Billy,' he said. 'Please let me explain the alleged crime.' I eagerly nodded and made myself comfortable on the floor.

'I was Christmas shopping alone in Mayfair when I remembered a very special date that was coming up, an important date in my fiancée and my diary. I needed to find an impressive gift, so I shopped around the beautiful jewel shops of the exclusive roads in the area. In one shop my eye filtered through the trays of diamonds and other precious stones, looking for that one fabulous rock that I could present to the love of my life.

'During my time in the shop, the salesman presented many trays of high-end gems, one after another. At one stage he turned around, and my hand was over my mouth because I was going to cough. He looked down at the tray in horror and informed both the other shop staff that a piece from the display was missing. Panic set in and they immediately locked the shop door and asked me if I had the missing jewel. I said "No, I have taken nothing". Then one younger staff member told my accuser to check the CCTV, and they quickly did. The only female member of staff stared into the screen like she was reading an interesting book. "He's swallowed it," she announced.

'"You're all crazy," I replied, but I could not leave the store, and then the salesman called the police and now I'm here.'

What an adventure, I thought. I bought Giuseppe's story – he was only coughing. He stood up and paced around the cell.

'What will my parents think?' he mumbled. I was thinking the same about mine. 'Billy, you take the bed and blanket now – I've sat down long enough.'

I moved onto the bed and laid out. We talked a little longer about the jewel shop, but Giuseppe was intent on hearing my life story and understanding exactly where I worked. He insisted that he would call me, and that we would meet up when we were both free again.

'You've been so kind and understanding, and my fiancée would love to see all your animals,' he said. At this point the cell door opened, and two police officers informed Giuseppe he was going to the hospital.

'At last,' I said to the police. 'His wrists could be broken.'

'He's going for X-Rays, but not on his wrists,' one of the officers laughed sarcastically. He marched my new friend out and banged the door shut on me.

I rolled over on the bed and pulled the blanket over my body, exhausted and grateful to stretch out. I started to fall asleep. While I was dozing, I felt something odd under the blanket. I picked it up and rolled it around in my hand, trying to work out what it was. My dreamy mind pictured a Murray Mint, or a Foxes Glacier sweet. Without further investigation, I popped it into my trouser pocket and fell asleep.

I was finally released hours later, long after the fur shop had closed, and I imagined my fellow activists would have packed up and gone home. To my surprise, two loyal mates, Laughing Janie and Soraya were still waiting for me. Janie was a living image of the masterpiece Flaming June by Flaming June by Frederic Leighton, with her glossy long red locks and soft pale skin. Soraya our blond bombshell was always turning the men's heads. The girls provided me with a drink, sweets and crisps as refreshments for my journey home and walked me to the station. There was no better company than these two great woman and time with them always guaranteed a smile on your face too. We exchanged a group hug and kisses at Charing Cross, and said our goodbyes as we parted for the next week or so. They disappeared into the mass of travellers, Janie's laughter ringing out behind them. Life returned to normal, and I thought that was the last I would ever hear from Giuseppe – how wrong I was.

It was late afternoon at work at the nursery school, when my boss came in and told me there was a call for me. She took over my class and I went to the phone. Imagine my surprise when I heard Giuseppe's voice, not a parent with a drama needing me. Giuseppe explained that I was a hard man to track down, but that he and his fiancée would love to take me out for dinner and repay my kindness.

'There's really no need,' I said. 'I'm just so happy you're well and that things got sorted out.

'We insist,' Giuseppe said. 'How would Friday night do?' So, the date was set, and I would finally find out the end to Giuseppe's terribly embarrassing mishap.

We met at Cranks in Carnaby Street, so I could show them how to eat kindly and advocate the vegan way. Maria was beautiful, tall and slim, and her future husband who stood holding her hand was also the picture of perfection. We greeted each other as if we were lifelong friends, and Giuseppe immediately began to complain about the coffee sold in non-Italian cafes, and how London had some serious catching up to do on the coffee front.

The amused-looking waiter took our order. My only thoughts on coffee drinking at the time were the bonus of dropping a few sugar cubes into my trouser pocket as a treat for Libby the pony at home. We ate the delicious food, and chatted about animal rights (of which Giuseppe and Maria had little knowledge), Italian politics (of which I had little knowledge), their stylish upcoming wedding and, finally, what happened to Giuseppe at hospital.

Beaming, he said, 'The hospital x-rayed my stomach under police guard, and of course there was nothing there! Crazy English people...they thought I'd swallowed a diamond the size of an impressive Italian olive, and would have waited for me to pass it?' The mystery remained as to what really happened to the missing magnificent Mayfair jewel. Our time ran out, as I needed to catch the last train. We'd all had a great night, and our unique friendship was born over the best cauliflower cheese in London, even if the coffee was poor. Friendships are made in the funniest of places.

Giuseppe, Maria and their beautiful family now support my actions for animals from afar, but nonetheless are still integral in my animal project's success. As we kissed goodnight Maria handed me an envelope with beautifully inscribed handwriting on the front: *With sincere thanks for the kindness you showed Giuseppe during his arrest.* She held my hand tight and kissed me goodnight. I guessed the contents of the envelope might be a donation for the animals, or maybe even a wedding invite.

As we began walking our separate ways, I tucked Maria's envelope deep into my trouser pocket of sugar cubes. There, I felt a strange object slightly bigger than the sugary rocks. I pulled it out, realising it was Giuseppe's double-wrapped Glacier mint from our time in the West End Central Police station.

'Giuseppe,' I called out, 'haven't you forgotten something?' He turned around with a surprised look on his face. I threw the covered candy into the air above him, shouting 'Catch!' Giuseppe looked up and firmly caught his prize in both hands.

'Crazy English people!' he sang aloud, then winked at me and walked off into the night.

Chapter Fourteen: Precious moments

Precious moments are etched into your life. They are your dearest memories. For me, these include my eldest niece Flun (Amy) being born just after 3pm on a Wednesday, just as I was going into an exam. I'd had to wait it out until the test was done before I could hear the exciting news of her arrival. Then, many years later, her marrying Adam and giving me a batch of incredible great-nieces and nephews. Times like hearing a friend once say: 'The Retreat, not just a place but a promise.' And how would I ever forget being handed my first rescue Dachshund Lovejoy at midday on the first of February with the Ronettes playing 'Be My Baby' on the radio, a heart-stopping precious moment. Another unforgettable precious moment when my parents renewed their wedding vows with us all there by their side on the island St Lucia in the Caribbean. Precious moments are the key to a happy and fulfilled life, that ensures burnout doesn't get you or finish you off. Then there are those more everyday acts of kindness that we all see everywhere.

I received a call from a woman called Marion who had returned from a holiday abroad to find a stray cow in her garden. *Did she say cat or cow? Oh my goodness, she really did say cow.* Marion had no idea where the blind Highland cow had come from but knew she couldn't stay. While Marion did the ring-around to find a rescue space because she was not having her shot as people suggested, she named the cow grazing her lawn Emma. It turns out Emma had been a stray living all alone in the local woods for years. Something must have spooked her out and she found sanctuary in the empty house. Due to her epic pair of horns and her being completely wild it took Lil, Neil and myself to herd her with a tennis net into the trailer, but not before she had galloped at high speed around the garden and exhausted us all. 'All in a day of precious moments,' I sighed. Emma settled well with our cows and became relaxed but never tame during her life with us.

Our home has become a pilgrimage for those wanting to find their precious moments. They come to support what we have created and ensure its legacy lives on well after we are all gone. I am more than happy to share my home with all who want to come and visit; it's a great resource for the conversion to kindness. It gives those who really care about what happens to animals a chance to breathe and see some real goodness. Be surrounded by animals who have escaped the systemic extermination of their living relatives. Behind every supermarket label there's a story of someone's life. Thankfully the very ones who escape tell a harrowing story of their families who weren't so lucky. My home restores people's faith, and our residents are living proof that animals have hopes and dreams too. We've even had a beautiful wedding and now a three-day festival in our meadows among our residents – paradise.

These residents include Sylvia the cow, a real precious moment who arrived at only twelve hours old – now a ginormous field puppy of five years old. A grown-up girl she may be, but one who still comes to her dad's voice when I call for my darling girl. We experience record years of visitors – now, ten thousand people come in the moments we are open, each having the chance to connect with the most precious of moments.

My husband and The Retreat's very own master chef Neil produces our best selling and actual size vegan Scotch egg, or 'welsh veggs' as I like to call them (Neil's welsh and a vegan). Our friend and patron, TV presenter

Jasmine Harman, brought home £30,000 of prize money from the TV show *The Chase*. Lacey, the failed polo pony who was to be shot, was rescued and taken to my sister Lil for some real love and fostering. Lacey gave us all the best gift when she gave birth to baby Spirit (named by my niece Darcy) on the 23rd July, the same birthday as my nephew Toby, who did some of the early caring for her. Precious moments come in all shapes and sizes and most of them will be a complete surprise. Just count on the magic of animals and your natural magnetism will provide the wonders.

It wasn't so long ago that I offered to do a transport run to reunite a rescue puppy with her mum. Little did I know, the pup's mother was now in Liverpool. On arriving at the kennels to collect the most gorgeous and cuddly of pups, I was given the postcode. I tapped it into our sat-nav, and Neil and I were shocked to learn that the destination was six hours away. We set off on the most tedious of transport runs with one motorway delay after another and even experiencing the QE2 bridge being closed. Finally, we arrived at the pup's new home at eleven o'clock at night. After seeing thrilled mum and pup's delight at being reunited we decided to get a hotel for the night. We fell on the bed exhausted and anticipated another nightmare of a journey back home the following day.

At breakfast we decided to take the scenic route back and leave out as many motorways as possible. This new route would include a stop at the old city of Chester, which neither of us had visited before. A bonus for us was that Chester had a Vbites eatery (one of the restaurant chain owned by vegan food pioneer, entrepreneur and record-breaking Olympian skier Heather Mills). The cathedral city of Chester with its grade-one listed walls did not disappoint and neither did Vbites, where I stocked up on food for the rest of our road-trip. Then we left behind the black-and-white painted medieval buildings and set off for home.

It was extremely cold, and there were a few signs of snowflakes falling. As we took the windy roads through the picturesque countryside, we came across a beautiful spot with a small space for parking, where we could take in the breath-taking views. Only one other car was braving the elements with engine still running. I got out and walked to the viewing point, where the driver of the lone vehicle called out his window to be careful because there was a tiny wild boar in the bushes and its parents wouldn't be happy if I disturbed them. Having reared wild boar orphans in the past, I was curious to have a peek.

As I crouched down and stared apprehensively into the undergrowth the small creature, barely able to stand, started to stumble and sway towards me. The other car pulled out of the parking area and drove off. I knew immediately that this was not a wild boar but a young domesticated piglet, potentially only two weeks old. With no idea how he'd managed to get here alone, I could only imagine he had been dumped – maybe even by the man now driving off. He made his was to me and pushed my trainer with his snout. With no hair and no body reserves to keep him warm, it wouldn't have been long before he perished. Without a second thought, I picked up the tiny baby and tucked him into my jacket, before returning to the car to show Neil.

Sometimes we just happen to be in the right place at the right time. Who knows what brought us together? It's like finding a four-leaf clover, spotting a rainbow or looking up at the night sky the same moment a shooting star breaks through the darkness. Is it your magic, your magnetism or a serendipitous moment in time? We drove home and I cuddled our priceless abandoned baby for the entire journey. If it hadn't been for our intrigue to visit the historical city of Chester (or, okay, the flavours of Vbites food), we never would have found the baby, so in the city's honour we named our new-found tiny friend Chester.

A very funny precious moment occurred when my friend Liz Varney and I were trapping feral cats for neutering in an old town in Greece. Once we collected the cats, we would take them back to the field surgery for the vet to neuter each one. As a visual form of identification to be sure the cats were neutered, the vet removed the point of the left ear. This showed the communities we worked in, along with the town's mayor, that a charity had help reduce the numbers. Usually this then prevented a crueller method being implemented.

Once the cats were off the operating table the cotton wool on the left ear was usually removed. Occasionally if a cat woke up quickly the cotton ball remained so no one was bitten. Most cats removed any signs of it whilst cleaning themselves, but during the release of one group of cats, one ran out of the basket with the fluffy white ball still on his ear. The old men sitting nearby drinking coffee laughed and laughed, and eventually waved Liz and I over. Their laughter was now hysterical, and Liz asked them what was so funny. The men then quietened down, and allowed the wisest and oldest to speak. He leaned in towards Liz.

'Since the beginning of time, animals have given birth, and if you think removing the top of an ear will stop cats having kittens you're mad.' The men continued to roll around with uncontrollable laughter, leaving us with no response to their wisdom. An important message to all is to create as many precious moments in life as possible, and fill your heart with them, for they fuel our soul.

Chapter Fifteen: Serendipity

The dictionary definition of serendipity is '*The occurrence and development of events by chance in a happy or beneficial way.*' So, kind of like a chance meeting. I have been so lucky to meet a few amazing people who were doing great things for animals, people and the planet in this way.

I was down a quiet lane in Eynsford, Kent trying to trap a wise injured Lurcher dog who had been living off the land and worrying some local sheep. So far, the dog had managed to evade capture by outsmarting me at every twist and turn. Roger the Dodger as I called him wanted desperately to be friends, but previous human interactions made him extremely cautious of us uprights. I put the tastiest treats in the trap and filled it with soft straw and newspaper, but nothing was enough even for this hungry boy. He would come within feet of me to smell what I had brought him each day with a wagging tail. A dog's tail never lies so you know you're halfway there if it's wagging when you're greeted by a canine.

This has been a great lesson for me. A mother and daughter duo used to come and clean my house, and there were never any wagging tails for them. The pair were immediately disliked by two of my long-term and very knowing dogs. No matter what I did to try and get the dogs to welcome them, they would instead emit a low growl with their tails beneath their legs, and disappear behind the furniture. At the time I found this incredibly strange, because I thought the two women were trustworthy – even scrupulously honest. I should have listened to my perceptive dogs' instincts and learned something from them. The dogs were right all along, and clearly trying to tell me something, but I didn't listen so ended up learning the hard way. If only I had a truth detector (a tail), I could rule the world.

Roger the Dodger was sleeping rough under an amazingly broad oak tree, having dug out his spot and curled up there when there was no one around. I had decided to start behaving like a dog and with minimal clothes on and no shoes or socks, I started to crawl around on all fours to get him playing with me and forget all his worries. The plan would be to get closer to the van each time and even with something tasty in the back of the van we'd both jump in and I'd close the doors, job done. It wasn't long before Roger was following the crazy half-dressed village idiot on all fours around like my best mate.

I crawled down the bank with an interested Roger behind onto the tarmac of the quiet lane. With Roger trotting along now by my side I downplayed my enthusiasm and pretended to sniff a tree. I then heard a car approaching. With all the exhausting hard work, sore knees and thorns embedded in my feet, Roger took off. The car slowed to a halt alongside me and the window came down, a rather bemused woman staring at me from inside. She asked me what I was doing and I explained the situation, trying not to sound like a madman. I told her that I had spent three weeks trying to catch a stray dog who had more wisdom running through his veins than Confucius did, so I had resorted to acting like his dog friend. The woman looked thoroughly thrilled, if not a little puzzled. Her reaction wasn't what I expected.

'You won't believe this,' she said, 'but my auntie is in a similar situation and is desperate to find help to catch another needy dog.' What are the odds of that? The world's quietest lane, and I got another rescue job. I gave the woman my number for her aunt to call me. Eventually the woman drove away, and I returned to my task of catching Roger who was now fast asleep in his dugout. I crawled under the tree alongside him, and he didn't get up. His eyes said it all; he now trusted me, and his tail gave a little wag. Rather than disturb him, I lay down beside him and gently placed the slip-lead over his head. I stroked his dusty coat and wiped the dirt from his eyes. When he was ready, we walked together to the van. It was a miracle – Roger was ready to be rescued.

That evening, with Roger settled in the kitchen I answered the phone to the woman's aunt who I'd heard about earlier.

'Is this Billy?' an excited voice said. 'Good, I'm Maureen. I hear you're good with dogs, and can help me with a sad little dog living on a golf course.'

I asked about the problem, and Maureen explained the situation in full detail. I agreed to help her, and because she was so desperate she asked me when I could do it.

'This weekend,' I replied.

'Okay, I'll get you a flight booked,' Maureen said.

'A flight booked?' I replied in shock. 'Where is this dog?'

'Didn't my niece tell you?' Maureen said. 'I live in Marbella.'

'Whenever an animal needs me, I'll be there,' I replied, and so Maureen booked my flight.

Two days later I flew into Malaga, not knowing Maureen from Adam. As I came through arrivals I saw a man holding a sign with my name on it. I waved to him and he politely greeted me: 'Good morning Mr Thompson, this way please.' *A chauffeur driven car all for me,* I thought. *This dog must be important.*

The Marbella sun was shining at its best as we sped along the highways. The car pulled up at a pair of impressive gates, which opened electronically to reveal a spectacular, enormous white Spanish villa nestled in the hills above Puerto Banús. With manicured lawns and finely clipped trees in large terracotta pots, the property looked like something from a Bond movie. From behind a fenced-off area I could hear the barks and yelps of dogs, and across the lawns beyond the paradise of a beautifully designed swimming pool, Maureen sat on a sun lounger waiting for me, dressed all in white. She came over and warmly welcomed me to Marbella, thanked me for my help and offered me a glass of chilled water.

I had no idea what I had let myself in for, and Maureen told me her schedule for the next forty-eight hours. Her friend, the Bond actor and animal lover Sean Connery and his wife were visiting to do a photoshoot for *Hello!* magazine to promote Maureen's animal rescue efforts.

Maureen's husband Bernard was the brother of Gordon White of Hanson and White, one of the UK's most successful takeover firms. Lord Hanson of Hanson and White had even been engaged to the beautiful Hollywood actress Audrey Hepburn. But in between her star-studded cocktail parties and visits from famous friends, Maureen was helping the strays of Puerto Banús. She was an animal lover with a huge heart. Maureen gave me my map, showing where I could find the first of the three trapping jobs that she needed help with. Nobody had managed it yet, she explained. I set off in her little van, which usually took the resident dogs to the beach each day, to trap my first dog.

My first assignment was Whitey the wild West Highland White Terrier, who was living wild on a golf course. This one was easy. Within the hour, he was in the cage trap on his way back to Maureen's. Shocked to see me back so soon she gave me my next job: mum and pups on building site. I shot over and within three hours mum and pups were also safety back with Maureen. I did wonder why I had come all the way to Spain for this, but Maureen insisted she'd had absolutely no luck and that I really was the man for the job. I had the rest of the afternoon to go and chill by the beach and enjoy the sunset.

The next day was my final job and instead of bringing Maureen home the dog she wanted, I caught three in the trap and returned with them. Maureen was so grateful she declared that when the famous photoshoot was done, she would take me wherever I wanted to go. I spent the rest of the afternoon playing with the newly rescued dogs until she was ready. Bond and his entourage smiled happily whilst holding the cutest of canines and Maureen waved to me, gesturing that it wouldn't be long before I got my reward. I told Maureen that all I wanted was some vegan ice cream – a rather tall order for Spain back then. To her credit, she knew exactly where to find it, and we drove to a Safeway supermarket in Gibraltar.

It wasn't long before I realised that not only did Maureen not have time for trapping due to her incredible social calendar, but that nobody had been shown how to use a trap properly. After a short lesson in trapping with Maureen's kind team, I left for the airport knowing my job was done.

My next chance meet ties in nicely with my reward of vegan ice cream. While immersed in a book on holistic medicine for animals (by the pioneering English herbalist Juliette de Baïracli Levy) I overheard a conversation with the chap sat in front of me. I was travelling on a plane bound for the wild and windy Island of Fuerteventura in the Canary Isles just off North Africa. The chap was in his eighties, and was pointing out in the most polite and gentle manner to the stewardess that his tray of in-flight food was not suitable for vegans. The frustrated and ill-informed member of cabin crew was arguing that this was what the man had requested, and there was no other option. The man refused to take the tray, and settled for nothing.

It was at a time when you didn't bump into many vegans, especially not sat next to you on a plane. I couldn't believe it as the same arrogant 'Trolley Dolly' then handed me the man's non-vegan meal. I also refused it, pointing out that butter and yoghurt were dairy and so not for me either. The woman snarled at me, thinking *What are the chances – two vegans on a plane at once?* I hope she's working now, with the vegan revolution taking place. I didn't get the chance to chat with the man and for the first few days I felt disappointed to have missed the opportunity to connect with him, but by a real fluke or a serendipitous intervention I spotted the grey-haired sprightly fella leaving a supermarket in town. We stopped the car and I got out and approached the man.

'Hi, I'm Billy,' I greeted him. 'I'm not a clairvoyant, but I do know you're a vegan. I sat behind you on the plane, and I heard you refuse your mile-high meal.'

'Yes,' the man replied. 'I'm Arthur, and yes I am a vegan.' We chatted for a while and decided to meet for drinks later at our villa.

That evening, Arthur and his companion arrived promptly with gifts of fresh island fruit from the market. Imagine my complete surprise when Arthur spilled the (soy) beans that he was the business owner of Plamil foods, *and* a vegan pioneer who had been a founding member of the UK Vegan Society – no less than Arthur Ling himself! Along with Donald Watson and a few others, they had created the word 'vegan' from the first three and last two letters of vegetarian, to create a new term for pure vegetarians. Founded in 1944, The Vegan Society was the oldest vegan organisation in the world. Arthur went on to explain that vegans during and after the war did not take any non-vegan foods allocated to them in their government ration books.

'It was a protest,' he explained. 'Even if we could have traded these "foods", it would have been wrong, and against all we stood for.' Never again would I complain about being offered only a limp salad in certain outlets at home. Arthur was an incredible human, full of kindness and knowledge, although a little pessimistic about the human race. I feel he would be surprised to see his word, *vegan,* being advertised on the side of city buses, spoken about at international climate conferences, and recognised as a protected belief in UK law. Vegan menus are in many high-street food outlets, some pioneering universities *only* serve vegan food, and you'll even find your average Joe Bloggs choosing a vegan meal in a steakhouse to offset his carbon footprint. And what would Mr Ling and Mr Watson have thought of the Greggs vegan sausage roll which took the media by storm, and all the airtime it gave to further the vegan movement?

I returned from this very memorable holiday where a most unsuspecting hero had sat in front of me. Not all superheroes wear capes, after all, and I thought there was no better accolade for such an inspirational man who had achieved so much. The next rescued bull calf to arrive at the centre would aptly be named Arthur. RIP two very special Arthurs.

Chapter Sixteen: Turn it into love

Every day at home, I deal with some rotten situations. These can include blocked visitors' toilets, new intakes full of bloodthirsty ticks, flat flies (look them up – they're like something from a horror movie), fleas and thousands of slimy maggots, horsefly bites, and a lot of disgusting sick. Animals arrive with smelly infected injuries covered in fly eggs that need to be dealt with before the vet can see them. I just knuckle down and get on with the day's challenge. It's at this point you realise the dream is not having an animal sanctuary, but the ultimate dream of animal liberation.

Thankfully all the 'yuck' is counteracted by animals recovering well and the amazing people I meet. Incredible people doing amazing things, like Lisa and Mark Kendrick whose friends went on holiday to the "paradise" island of Mauritius to find out it was a nightmare for animals. When a sick little puppy who was later called Will arrived and needed desperate help, they called Lisa to save the little guy. This pup was the catalyst to something very special. The Kendricks set off an amazing course of events where Lisa and Mark, with the group they then set up, 4 Paws Rescue & Relocation International, have rescued and found homes for over one thousand dogs – incredible.

Every action has a reaction, so it's always best we choose a positive one. A positive decision will be better for you mentally and physically. Being kind is a positive for those animals who literally have no one fighting for them. We now know that if the world's pollinators were to disappear so would humankind but if the boot were on one of the many insects' feet, their world would only be a better place.

Don't listen to the farming industry's propaganda

about farmers loving their animals and treating them like 'family pets'. Love is the strongest of emotions, and everyone who really loves something genuinely works hard to ensure their safety and longevity. Art collectors would not destroy their beloved artefacts, nor would the classic car enthusiasts who worship their vehicles ever let any harm befall these inanimate objects. Yet farmers send their beloved babies and 'spent' animals – all sentient beings – to the slaughterhouse or worse, send them off as live exports to far-off lands.

The claim that the UK has some of the highest animal welfare standards in the world is oxymoronic to the point of being ludicrous. Laws have to be enforced to be effective, and with the scale of animal farming operations there is no way this would ever be possible. It's no different to the lack of legal commitment to police fox hunting now it's been banned.

A sheep farmer recently argued that sheep farming is great for the environment, and that there are certain areas like the Welsh and Scottish hills where you can only farm sheep. With a simple bit of research, I found the opposite to be true. Hills would be appropriate places for growing and managing woodland, a material that we mostly import. And thanks to George Monbiot's book *Feral*, I learned that landslides are worsened by sheep grazing, because they compact and erode the soil, preventing the trees and shrubs whose roots might have otherwise fixed the slope from growing. It's even claimed that 'sheep have done more damage to Britain's environment than all the building that has ever taken place'. This is without the evils behind the husbandry of keeping such numbers of these kind and friendly animals. With farmers already owning the assets of farms and equipment, then drawing on huge subsides of taxpayer money (unlike any other business), they are in an extremely privileged position to change to a kinder compassion-led economy; one without the use of animals.

People of the Faroe Islands will routinely drive to shore groups of pilot whales and dolphins to hack them to death as a pastime. There is no need to behave like barbarians in a century where such atrocities should be expelled to the history books of shame. Why can't they swim with these magnificent creatures instead, and show the watching world a leap from evil to kindness? This unnecessary violent end to the life of such peaceful creatures is a blot on their very beautiful landscape and showcases their depravity instead.

We need to stop looking at animals like they are less than us, they are just different. If you really knew animals you would not harm them, or let them be harmed in your name. An amazing book which supports this way of thinking is Jeffrey Mason's *The Pig Who Sang to the Moon,* the very first book exploring the emotional lives of farmed animals, and a must-read in the face of institutional prejudice against animals. *Extraordinary Insects* by Anne Sverdrup-Thygeson is another incredible book which emphasises the vital role insects play in our increasingly fragile ecosystem – a real slap in the face of those arrogant parents who let their children step on snails and squash ants. Teach your children to turn it into love instead. A kind child is the best child.

Good people are magnets to great people and so make good connections for good ideas. When I'm at The Retreat and we have the visiting public in I can see this before my own eyes. The Retreat is a kindness hub for those like-minded people; we meet, connect and become friends. Before I wrote *Earth Boy,* a visitor came and introduced himself to me.

'Hello, I'm Cliff,' he said, 'and if you ever need any

advice with writing or publishing, my daughter's over there – she may look fifteen but she's actually in her twenties – and could be very useful.' So, our friendship was born over our love for animals, a simple trip out from London to meet rescued animals had brought us together. Most surprisingly to me, a year later I handed the manuscript of *Earth Boy* over to the amazing Isabel Martin (without any grammar) and she so swiftly and kindly brought my book *Earth Boy* to life. In gratitude I named a newly arrived cow Isabel in her honour, after discussing with her dad what would be appropriate payment for such help. Cliff (Martin) her Dad who introduced us has now written a fantastic children's book called *Help! Children Have Taken Over the World*, which kindly supports The Retreat too.

There is also my dear and inspiring friend Angie Hamp whose brainchild The Neuter Project Clinic at The Retreat came from her idea of reducing the tens of thousands of unwanted litters of puppy and kittens and smaller domestic animals every year. I came up with a suitable building for an onsite registered veterinary clinic and sharing the love its now fully operational; a free facility for all charities to use.

A day at The Retreat can be summed up by the kind actions of a few humans we couldn't do without. Jan (seventy-six) on the horse team, who also cleans the visitors' toilets so they're suitable for a queen. Eric Gear (eighty-eight), a real gentleman and fellow whiskey drinker who likes the brand Highland Park, who regularly visits and buys a ton of books from the thrift shop and donates them back on his next visit – and still doesn't leave without putting a note in the collection box. Zoe and her son Charlie (sixteen) who regularly visits us because one day Charlie's going to have his own pig rescue centre. Then there's Phil Mild who arrives in his Silver Shadow for a vegan bacon sandwich and puts a smile on everyone's face. This is why we say 'friendships are made and never forgotten at The Retreat'.

As writing this book comes to a close and I look forward to a well-deserved glass of Chianti and finishing reading the book *Rivers Apart* (a captivating love story) by author Nora Rose, I count my blessing for being a custodian of such a project, The Retreat, a kindness hub; my home. It's more than a job (even if unpaid), it's the beat that works my heart. Now with the world in a real mess, the climate emergency, the unjust war in Ukraine, the UK's cost of living crisis, four British prime ministers since David Cameron, there must be some good news...At last, people are waking up to the real cost of the 'meat' on their dinner plate.

Veganism is good for the farmed animals, wildlife, future generations, your carbon footprint and of course your health. By simply going vegan you are cutting out the high levels of antibiotics feed to fish and animals from your diet. It's not surprising that we are facing an antibiotic shortage, when vast quantities are still used in animal farming in the UK and across Europe. Farmers may even use antibiotics classed as 'highest priority critically important' for humans by the World Health Organisation. A staggering sixty-six percent of all antibiotics are used on farm animals.

A great week to end *The animal in me* comes with the arrival of seven saved beagles. The beagles' freedom was negotiated by The Beagle Freedom Project (BFP), who do amazing work. These docile and gentle dogs had all spent years in a cruel testing facility in Spain and were facing euthanasia but were rescued in the nick of time by BFPUK. I witnessed their first kind interactions with humans and saw the joy of grass beneath their paws. So, in the deeply poignant words (of another troubled time) inscribed inside Josephine Bonaparte's wedding ring from Napoleon, I leave you with '*Au destin*' (To Destiny).

The end

Acknowledgements

All those darling animals who changed my destiny for the better and the present residents of The Retreat. My husband Neil, Mum, Dad and my little sis Lil. My managers Rose and Scott. My PA Kerrie and my right-hand woman Dr Susan Bauer.

The farm team: Sorrell, Sam L, Sarah N, Morag, King-Ken, Anna & Marco, Anna Birkman Martin, Don, Emily, Amanda, Erin, Heidi, James, Roy, Jo, Charley & Ryan, Annie & Chris and Carl.

The Bird Team: Dave and Hatty.

The Horse Team: Gina, Vicky, Sue, Kate, June, Tania, Jo & Davey, Carl, Lori and Rebecca.

Treatment Team, Amelia, Sarah Philips.

Cat Team Heidi, Sophie, Nicki and Zoe.

Shop teams Jo, Sarah Z, Shining-Sandra. Ross and Donna.

Cafe team: Chris Fosbury, Emma, Eppy, Sara Starkey, Jo, Cameron.

Maintenance team: Dave Stephenson, Ben Pryer, Lewis, Peter Reynolds, Les Holness.

The Neuter Project Clinic: Angie Hamp at the helm, vets and nurses. The Flair Foundation Feeders: Carol and Jackie.

The Retreat's Board of Trustees Lil, Cara, Mandi, Alex and Chloe.

Pat and Peter French. Richard Thoburn. Eddy French. June Mahoney and Tony Whitehead. Gabi and Hans Keller. Danuta Mayer. Andrea Charlwood. Regan and Jerry. Annie, Roy and Emma (AIN). PJ. Pantelis and Evelina. Jeneen Schive. Colette Marshall. Scarlet, Beagle

Ambassador. Mobius Loop. Squirrel Mummies. Jasmine Harman. Hayley at Pet-Supermarket. Alison Hardy and family. Lesley CW and Sharon. Alison Dave Vicky and George Baker. Kate Owens.

The Alpha Team Sally, Mark Scott Kat Harrison and John. Jannette and Shona Fergus. Sally Queen of Raffles. Carman and Rob of Mad Ideas. Cathrine and Katie at Green Kitchen. Books by Nora Rose (AKA Jo Stephenson), Woodlark. Brian Saville. Teresa Wildflowers Favours. Rocky Benderskum, Isabel and Cliff Martin. Jo and Jason at Ethel loves Me. Annmarie of Shed loads of Love. Elizabeth Tim and sheep. Maggie Dixon. Rebecca and Kate Wild Kind Heart festival team. Jodie and Phill. Becky Matt and Jake Davis. Jill and Phill Giles. Jade & Paul, Kylie on show. Harry and Mark aka Vegan Squirrel. Corin lee. Greta and Paul. Our great neighbours Mel and Gary Smart. Every single one of our visitors and donors. Jan Waples. Tow-Bar-Sue. Indie Angel. Heathcliff. Derek Summers. Ben Savil. Zena Watson. Chris and Sylvia. Heather and Fiona Mills, Vbites. Animal Aid. Leigh Mulley. Vets RW Equine, Badgers Oak, Herondens. The Maureen Grey Foundation. Sam at Tail Blazers Mobile Dog Groomers.

Lyn Williams RIP, Happy Dogs Rescue and family. Margaret Aldridge RIP, Colne Valley Animal Rescue. John Potts RIP, Swans & Friends and Dauphine Robinson RIP, the bird lady of Coney Hall.